Tim-BERRR!

Pine Logging in the
Big Fork River Country

VOLUME I

Benhart Rajala

Some historical information came from published works by Agnes Larson, Grace Lee Nute, Pierre Burton, Robert Pike, Stewart Holbrook, and others.

Cover photo: Ben Rajala Collection.

Second Printing: October 1992

Design: Corinne A. Dwyer

Prepared by North Star Press of St. Cloud, Minnesota.
Printed in the United States of America by Versa Press, Inc. of East Peoria, Illinois.

Acknowledgments

My grateful thanks to all the friends and neighbors who shared their memories with me: Charles Bibeau, Leonard Dickinson, Jim Reid, "Dutch" and Len Knotts, Hadley Malvig, A D Moors, David Patrow, Earl Peloquin, Fred Peloquin and Frank Werthner, along with several others. I couldn't have done it without you.

I would have liked to have included all the men I knew in woods work, but it would never be possible. All have helped in shaping my thinking and have helped to make this recollection.

There are several living loggers whose stories have had a big part in the development of the Big Fork Valley logging area, whose work I haven't included: Carl Dahlberg, Theodore Lovdahl, Lyndon Kendall, David Patrow, to name a few. They have their own stories to tell. I did not want to infringe on any history of theirs, nor that of my old friend Jim Knight, who (I think) has another book in his packsack.

I hope those of you who read this book will not judge it as history, though I have tried to be as accurate as possible, and I have confidence in the information given to me by those whose clear, vivid recollections have helped make a picture of logging as it was in the good old days, gone but not forgotten. Again, my thanks to all of you who helped.

Benhart Rajala
written in 1979

Contents

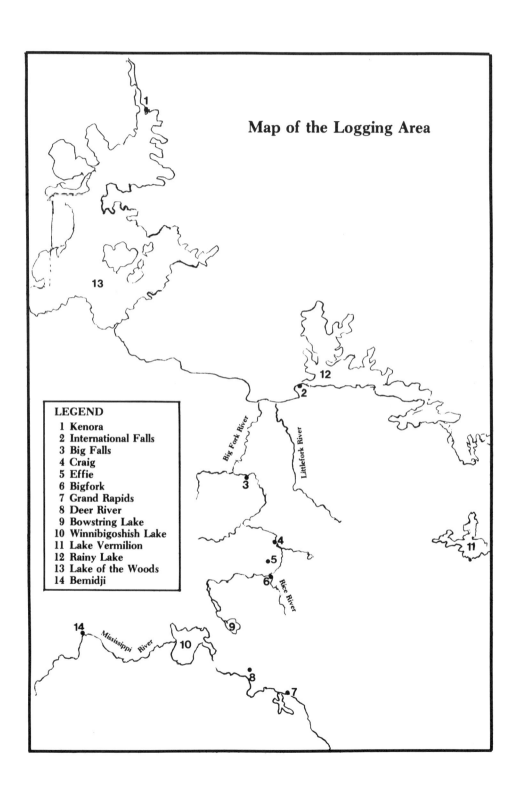

Map of the Logging Area

LEGEND
1 Kenora
2 International Falls
3 Big Falls
4 Craig
5 Effie
6 Bigfork
7 Grand Rapids
8 Deer River
9 Bowstring Lake
10 Winnibigoshish Lake
11 Lake Vermilion
12 Rainy Lake
13 Lake of the Woods
14 Bemidji

Big Fork River

Littlefork River

Rice River

Mississippi River

1

Shadows in the Timber

Paul Bunyan was the greatest lumberjack in the world, and the biggest. When he was born, it took five giant storks working in relays to deliver him to his folks. He was so big they had to use a lumber wagon for a baby carriage, and his mother made him a little jacket with wagon-wheels for buttons. He was often hungry, and when he'd holler for food it was so loud it would blow all the frogs out of the pond.

Once upon a time, in America, everybody was a lumberjack.

This was just a fact of life. Standing timber, walls of it, seemingly endless, were the first thing the Pilgrims saw when they anchored at Plymouth Rock. It was something Europeans had never experienced. Naturally, it had to be cut.

Before that, Captain John Smith had his dandies chopping down trees (and it is recorded that they used much lumberjack language, for which the doughty Captain devised the punishment of pouring a cupful of cold water down the offender's sleeve for each bad word used. This may have been effective at the time, but since then, colorful language has been accepted as the lumberjack's natural speech). Even earlier, Leif Erickson in 1000 hauled timber back to Greenland from America. Chopping down trees was the American Way.

Well into the present century, the forest was an economic fact paramount in the life of each American pioneer. It represented security: from the forest came the material for his home, and fuel to keep his family warm. (Even if they burned coal, they needed "kindling.") It was both friend and enemy. Standing, it provided cover for attacks by the Indian whose land had been stolen, as well as food and game from nature. It had to be subdued before he could sow his crops, but in doing so it made fences to keep his livestock safe and establish his territory. With all that, it provided a livelihood. Cities and towns back east were crying for timber. So it was a fine thing that the forests of America were inexhaustible. The men who reaped the harvest from them were admired, not reviled.

Presently, there was a whole aggregation of men who followed the timber, cutting it down, sawing it up, and hauling it to market—the shanty boys and their bosses. Nobody minded. What did it matter? Everyone knew that the forests would last to the millenium.

Hindsight being clearer than foresight, we now know how mistaken that was. But to the settlers, the trees were actually a detriment. They wanted to farm, to raise much-needed food. They were happy to find some market and return for the "tall weeds" which had to be cut down and removed.

It makes a man groan, these days, to hear of lush stands of hardwood—including walnut and butternut and chestnut, the rare jewels of the forest—being grubbed and felled in windrows and burned as waste, to clear the land for the plow. "Letting the daylight in" was essential; the sun's warming rays energized the land.

Down came the trees, and the immediate needs were met as a consequence. Farm buildings, town houses and business establishments were constructed from these excellent materials, handy and cheap; and many are standing today that are 150 years old. There are bridges resting on chestnut piling in the Eastern States believed to be over 200 years old.

It wasn't all bad. Most of the timber materials were put to important good use, and without this bounteous supply of forest products the early settlers wouldn't have made it.

The truth is, the old white pine was mature, and had to go, one way or another through natural causes: rot, fire, wind. The best thing happened when men with axes and saws came along, salvaging the old stuff and putting it to use. However, there are many sides to this picture. Some scholars believe the decaying forest matter is necessary to regenerate a new crop.

In any event, the idea of cutting timber to make lumber which could be sold for a nice profit grew naturally. It became a full-fledged business in Maine (which wasn't a state until 1820), and then leaped westward after the Civil War to encompass the forests of Michigan, Wisconsin, and Minnesota. By the time the Big Pine was felled in Minnesota, logging methods were almost a science, and there was a special breed of men who pitted their strength against the forest: the lumberjacks.

Most of Minnesota was logged in the tradition of the shanty-boys, as the loggers from the "pineries" of the East swung through, cutting their wide swath. In no time at all, the forest was gone. But there is a part of the state north of the Continental Divide, where the rivers flow northward, which was the lumberjack's last stand before he took the inevitable leap to the West Coast. In this area, virgin timber stands persist even now. Here settlement began with the traditional style of logging, and saw the transition from the struggle of men against the forest to the new era of soulless machines. With the advent of automation, the lumberjack became an endangered species. He is a Vanishing American. The way he lived and worked is a thing of the past.

Only a few of the Old Guard remain, and these are mostly in nursing homes. But their memories are filled with the sparkle of a life spent in surmounting hardship and danger. They challenged the wilderness, in days of tough chances, close shaves, and bitter, unremitting hardship, and they are proud of it. What's more, their stories are links in a chain that began far before their time.

Who were the first to lay their axes to the timber in the lands that sloped toward the Arctic?

A steady stream of logs floated down the Bigfork and Littlefork Rivers, and Upper Rainy waters, in early 1880, following the twisted course to the Rainy and thence rafted across Lake of the Woods to Rat Portage. Mills there were slashing out the rough planks and timbers needed for the Canadian railroad.

This was during the furious construction period when the Canadians were putting forth a great effort to stitch the two Canadas together by means of a railway. There was no other way—the far-flung lands of the West could barely communicate by packets of mail carried via voyageur's canoe. It took three months or a year for a letter to travel from Montreal to Winnipeg and on to Western Canada, passed by the swift-paced canoemen.

Captains of Industry in Eastern Canada were faced with the problem of introducing progress and commerce, "opening up the lands," through the impassable region north of the Great Lakes, across the fertile prairies, through the mineral-rich Rocky Mountains and on to Vancouver. The only way was to build a railroad connecting Western Canada with the East, and soon. Otherwise there were threats by the British Columbians to join with the Oregon territory and form a new nation— "Oregon, B. C."

The Canadian government, after a series of hot Parliamentary battles, settled the issue. The decision was made, at a great cost in dollars, and superhuman efforts of muscle, knowhow, and fortitude, to build the Canadian National. The last spike was driven barely twelve years after the American Union Pacific was completed.

The race was on! Settlers poured into the Western states and provinces. The building requirements of the stream of new inhabitants emigrating west were immense. Some economical material, easily accessible, would serve best.

Lumber and timber were urgently needed, beginning in the 1870s, for the construction of the Canadian transcontinental railway. Their main problem was getting around Lake Superior, over the rough, rocky terrain of the Pre-Cambrian Shield, where the tough, hard granite turned the drill bits and other tools dull so rapidly it made railroad progress almost impossible. Timber was the answer—for trestles and bridges crossing depressions or precipices.

The timbered regions of the Rainy River drainage held a good supply of pine, cedar, tamarack, and spruce to answer the purpose. The Big Fork and Littlefork valleys had some of the biggest and best. In many places along the rivers there were huge old white pine stands, unmolested by the pestilences of wind and fire. They were called "cork pine," differentiated from the smaller second growth. The only main difference I could ever tell was that this wood is from old trees, and of a corky, or seemingly softer substance. Besides, it is darker, somewhat creamy-orange in color, and has small wavy lines or sometimes curls in the grain. The wood is much lighter in density, the logs floating high in the water. This made for ideal driving down the rivers—rarely would they ever sink. It was soft-textured, easy-sawing, ideal milling wood. Due to its aged-in preserving qualities, this timber was choice, and much sought-after. The Norway pine, cedar, tamarack, and spruce were used, also, whenever they were accessible.

This timber, being within easy reach of the main watercourses in an area crisscrossed with streams and lakes, was quite naturally chopped down first. "Cant-hook loggers" went up the rivers, never straying far from the banks. Bankside logs were cut, and rolled or handspiked into the river by men mostly nameless, though a Cameron is known to have been among them. Along the Big Fork River men set up rollway skids of small poles laid down, and the big logs were rolled down the slopes right into the water. In this manner ambitious brawny men could do the whole logging job, with little more than their own hand tools and efforts. So they lugged into this big wilderness their packs: blankets, small tools, some rice, beans and tea, along with a rifle and their trusty axes; they built log huts where both timber and game were plentiful and for free, and they were in business.

Some word of this eventually reached the proper authorities. U.S.

timber agents were dispatched to investigate. One of these, J. S. Wallace, wrote of this trip in 1890. He stopped at a Loper and Rumery Camp sixty-five miles west of Tower—either the Farm Camp at Deer Creek, or west by Muldoon on the Big Fork River. From there he went on snowshoes to Rainy River and Lake of the Woods. He found the evidence of depredations, he wrote, saying, "Close along the boundary line, from Pine Creek east to Buffalo Point" (on Lake of the Woods, where in 1823 Bigsby found remains of a trading post) "there has been extensive trespass, but not of late years." This indicates older timber cuttings than were being done in the 1880's for purposes of Canadian railroad development, or building of communities in Minnesota and the Dakotas.

Wallace wasn't the first. A Canadian citizen, in 1882, warned of the depredations, and United States sent an investigator named Webster Eaton in 1883. It seemed the government sent somebody to nose into it every year, and after these dedicated men endured near-death by freezing, drowning, or murder by irate timber robbers, their reports lay in the files and nothing was done.

The Morris Act stopped most of these depredations, and by 1910 the United States Government was recovering revenues from stumpage, and repaying the Indians for lands and timber ceded. Without this early ambitious lumbering activity along the northern rivers, the progressive settlement of both the Canadian and United States west would have been much slower, or, in some instances, nearly impossible.

CANT HOOK

Ironically, the trespasses in the Big Fork and Littlefork valleys which amounted to 85,000,000 board feet yearly between 1880 and 1900 was a situation wherein the American logging companies assisted the Canadians by stealing the timber on American soil and selling it to Canadian mills. Then other Americans often bought the cheap lumber back.

My contention has always been that it didn't matter too much. At the time, it was the cheapest way to get the timber out of the region. The overripe trees had to be cut, and had very little value then. The greatest wrong was that they took too much too fast, and much of it not yet clearly ceded by treaty from the Indians. Yet it stands as an amazing feat of the great efficiency experts of their time.

The most baffling thing about the period from 1880 to about 1910 is the amount of pine that was taken out of the Big Fork River valley. If 50,000,000 board feet were taken as an average annual production, multiplied by thirty years, the result is 1,500,000,000 board feet. That is a lot of timber. Then add at least two times that amount for the Littlefork, Black Bay, Rainy Lake and Vermilion River, and LacLaCroix regions, and you have a total of 4,500,000,000 board feet of timber on log drives to the mills along the Rainy River and Lake of the Woods to Kenora. All of the approximately ten mills sawing lumber from these logs at this time were on Canadian soil.

The ruins of the old camps were visible for a long time. Mike Guthrie, who became Minnesota's first forest ranger in 1911, told me of an old trail going west from Farm Camp, along the north side of Deer Creek, then along the Big Fork River to what was later called Helm's bridge. There, he said, in the mouth of a ravine was a second-growth thicket of popple. Nearly hidden by the trees were the outlines of an old logging camp, with overgrown pine stumps in the surrounding hills. He had no doubt this was the Loper and Rumery camp mentioned in N.B. Wharton's government report of 1888.

But who were the ghostly cutters who logged even earlier, leaving the evidence of cutting that Wallace thought was old?

Gray-haired old men talked to me about logging before their time. One aging man told of seeing old choppings along the Big Fork. He believed the axe-work had taken place at least fifty years before he had traveled the river, in the 1890's, placing it at 1840 at the latest. He pondered on the mystery—large pine trees having been chopped down, and only clear portions of the tree taken for logs, then squared somewhat.

He noted that the timbers seemed to have been very long, and two-and-a-half to three feet in diameter.

Only one explanation seems to fit these facts. It can't be documented, but it's been told by thoughtful men since time immemorial. The story has its roots in the eastern colonies, where the tall straight white pine was discovered by shipbuilders to be ideal mast timber. It was far superior to the Baltic Fir, being taller and lighter. So all such standing timber was reserved for the King, and marked with a "broad arrow" which theoretically the colonists were supposed to respect (though they showed about as much respect as a fox for a handy chicken). When the colonies became states, national spirit and unlimited domestic markets made them thumb their noses at the King's need for mast timber, just when Great Britain was at the pinnacle of its expanding sea power. When masts could no longer be got by his "broad arrow," the King turned to the men of the forest who knew where there was a fresh supply. The border between the two countries west of the Great Lakes was nebulous; perhaps the King still felt that this land belonged to the Crown. In any case, the needs of the "Great White Fleets" must be met.

It is thought that the timbers cut along the rivers were floated all the way to Hudson Bay, and there loaded on ships bound for Merrie Olde England. Sounds incredible, doesn't it? And yet, it fits.

Val Angell, a very respected man and an all-around good logging boss, had memories that confirmed the legend. He had seen the old pine tree choppings early in 1900, and had heard old men talk around the campfires. With his brother, later in the United States Forest Service, he had found, some fifteen or twenty miles below Big Falls, the outline of a decayed building. The dirt banked around the walls showed the shape and size distinctly, and he described it as quite large. Growing out of the center of these remains was a white pine tree about eighteen inches in diameter at breast height, which would be approximately a hundred years old. "The cuttings there were very old," he said.

On the Sturgeon River, a large tributary to the Big Fork, about fifteen miles west of Big Falls, I met a Mr. Stein who was still living in his log homestead house, built by his parents in 1901 when he was an infant. As he and his brothers grew, they explored the woods around their home. They discovered, along the bank of the river, the outline of an old log cabin, built of burr oak, all ax-chopped. There was no mark of a saw.

Roaming in the "pine islands" several miles north (low hills that rise out of spruce and tamarack swamps) they discovered several smaller "dugout" cabins, still intact, with roofs that shed water. These had been built on a slope, and excavated to a depth of only three or four feet. They were rudely made, by falling two ten-foot pine trees parallel to each other about six feet apart, into the hill. The stumps held the soil in place to prevent caving. The top of the front wall and back were made from six-foot logs notched into the long ones. Under these timbers, the walls were made of split cedar logs, tightly fit together. The roof was also constructed of split cedar, on a ridge pole to give some slope. Birch and cedar bark covered it, with a top layer of what appeared to be peat.

There was a door, of rived plank, held in place with wood hinges and latch, and a small hole in the top to let in air and light. No stove or chimney existed. Inside, however, were shiny black rocks, and a similar pile was outside. The boys deduced that they were a source of heat— a hot fire outside heated the rocks, which were carried inside on forked sticks, to warm the cabin.

On the roof grew an eighteen-inch-diameter white pine tree. The roots spread out and down on the outside of the cabin in such a way as to support itself and at the same time protect the structure.

Years later, when Mr. Stein had grown up, he left the country for a long period. When he returned, he found that loggers had cut over the area. Had anyone seen the cabin? he wanted to know. No, they said. The cutting had been done when the snow was very deep. But he could still find the place.

Who were the men who had made the cabins? Very likely voyageur trappers. The time they could have been inhabited could be at best approximated by the growth of the white pine trees. We might guesstimate the age of the harvested trees to be eighty to a hundred years, sawlog size. This would place the time of habitation from 1800 to 1820 or 1830, which coincides right along with much of the voyageurs' activity in the fur trade.

The voyageurs certainly found the timber resource of the inland empire. The first log cutting in Rainy River country was done by their axes, building the trading posts and forts of the Northwest Company, Hudson Bay Company, and other fur trading enterprises. Many of these men were highly skilled in the use of axes and other tools used in boat building and carpentry; putting up buildings; main stores, meeting hall, quarters for officials and clerks, as well as barracks for soldiers and voyageurs.

CANT HOOK

The French used a unique corner to hold log walls together, instead of the commonly-known notched corners used in New England. They placed a corner post log upright in each corner. These logs were large enough to be grooved in such a manner as to hold the ends of the wall logs upright. The wall logs were squared, or flattened on the top and bottom surface, with such precision that little chinking except moss was used.

The squared logs with mortised ends were lowered into the grooves of the corner posts, "locked in." With the weight of the roofs resting on the walls, logs were compressed to a tight fit. Few nails, if any, were used: instead, wood dowels or pegs held timbers where necessary. Roofs were built of heavy split planks or logs, sturdy and durable, and covered with whatever came handy—birch bark, cedar bark, or shakes. The heavy timber had a good insulating value; consequently the fireplaces kept the occupants warm and comfortable in spite of the long, cold winters.

Voyageurs were not true lumberjacks, since they cut only what they needed themselves, and valued the standing timber as a habitat for fur-bearing animals. But they are worthy forerunners, being also men who ignored personal comfort and took little thought of the future, living cheerfully in the most miserable conditions and accepting hardship and bitter physical toil as their normal lot. And their footsteps in the timberland were first.

They were picked for their strong, short legs, strong backs, endurance, and ability with a paddle, along with good singing voices that lent color and excitement. They were men of action, carrying out the arduous tasks involved. Above all, it was imperative to know how to handle their watercraft in whatever circumstances they encountered.

They were dashing, jaunty men who propelled the great Montreal canoes, the forty-foot long birchbark baskets weighing three hundred pounds, capable of transporting five-ton loads up the Great Lakes to Grand Portage or Fond du Lac. From there they took their twenty-five foot "canot du nord," with a capacity of three thousand pounds plus crew, racing westward through unknown waters. Many places in northern Minnesota still carry names given them by the early voyageurs.

They built their own winter quarters from timber they found in the region, with axes. Two types of axes were used. The Hudson Bay style, a single-bit axe with a flare one way, was basic. The other was a broad style, with blade flared both ways, somewhat heavier. Both had flat heads to use in hammering. Some small saws, chisels, sharp knives, awls, and augurs made up the tool kit of this pre-lumberjack axe-man. Like the lumberjacks, he was willing to do anything, go anywhere, for any length of time required by the expedition. Homesickness is not an occupational disease in the forests.

One such man left home in Trois Rivieres when only sixteen, hearing as he paddled off with his canoe-mates the sound of church bells ringing to announce the baptism of a girl of the parish. Many adventures followed in the sixteen years that he spent in the forest; he was captured by Indians and held in a cave near St. Anthony Falls; he traveled up the Mississippi to Lake of the Woods, and westward across many waters to the "shining mountains."

Incidentally, the young voyageur returned to his home parish a man of wealth, and married the girl who had been baptized on the morning of his journey's start.

One expedition he described to his descendants—possibly the Fraser expedition—left from Winnipeg into the wild northwestern regions by way of the Saskatchewan River. They built posts in this new land, all the way to the mountain wall. There they left their canoes, crossed the mountains, and reached the headwaters of a fast, tumultous river. Large Balm-of-Gilead trees stood here. These they hollowed out, fashioning dugout boats. By leaving the bottom wood thicker, these became very stable craft, nearly impossible to tip over. In these cumbersome yet seaworthy things they descended this unknown river. Through the unnavigable rapids they swiftly shot the course to the sea, realizing as they went the impossibility of their return by water. They struggled back seven hundred miles on foot over rugged mountain trails to where they had cached their canoes and goods.

In Prince George, British Columbia, stands a large stone memorial to Simon Fraser and his nineteen men, who descended the Fraser River in 1808, two years after Lewis and Clark reached the Oregon Coast by way of the Columbia River.

While cruising timber in the Fraser River country, I paused in wonderment as I peered over the rim into the yawning chasms of Hope Canyon. I wondered how the brave souls dared risk all, while dashing through those rocky, treacherous, cascading currents. Only the bravest and best would dare try.

The voyageurs were not only axe-men themselves; they were fathers of many later lumberjacks who followed the woods.

One of these that I knew was Prisque Peloquin, who told me the voyageur story above. He was born in 1865, in the early French settlements near St. Paul, and grew up with the stories of the vast wild regions in the north—LacLaPluie, Koochiching, and the Bowstring, with the endless forests of pine trees. He came to the Bigfork woods in 1892.

There he found winter work for the Keewatin Company logging camps. He helped build camps, worked as a faller, and built bateaus and sacking boats as well as wanigans for use on the log drives.

The bateaux and wanigans had to be built new each spring. Once they went downstream, they were never brought back, for they were too heavy and cumbersome to force against the current, and could never have been maneuvered through the falls and rapids. The bateaux were built with heavy planking bottoms, clinker style, with a keel, and pointed at both ends. Side walls were heavy shiplap, to three-foot gunwales. The craft was six feet wide at the beam, and twenty-four feet long or longer. Sacking boats were square-built, flat-bottomed, of heavy planking with two-and-a-half foot gunwales and sloped-up ends, about five feet wide and twenty feet long.

The wanigan was a houseboat on a scow, and was used on log drives most importantly to transport the cook and supplies, and sometimes as sleeping quarters for the men. It had the ever-present wood-burning cook stove, a minimum of cooking utensils, tin dishes and supplies of food; hams, bacon, potatoes, coffee, and whatever was needed to last to the next supply point. The size was according to the number of men in the crew, and a drive might have more than one wanigan. Of two-inch planking, flat bottomed, with the ends sloped upwards, it was approximately twenty-eight feet long and eight or ten feet wide. The top of the gunwale was three feet above the double floor, with rough board walls forming a rude shelter, and a roof. Doors opened at each end, and a short deck was provided at both bow and stern, for steersmen. When the wanigan was passing through fast water, four men with poles (one at each corner) assisted, while the steersman plied a long oar in the center of the stern. If bunks were built, they were the simplest possible.

Most of the men who worked in these early camps were anonymous, and little is known of them as individuals. However, one of the earliest who made an appearance in the area in 1887, Damase Naveux, remained to become a settler. Some of his exploits may be recounted here.

"Uncle Tom," as he was called, spent little time at the camps, but was on good terms with the operators and men from the time he established himself at the foot of a pine-covered hill swooping down to the Big Fork River. From his cabin he dispensed the hospitality of the north — having a few chickens, a small still, and an extra room or two, his outpost became a popular stopping place for Indians, cruisers, and lumberjacks and company men alike. When Billy Clair of the Clair and Myers camp was down with smallpox in 1901, he was nursed back to health at Uncle Tom's. Cruisers paused there for a last convivial evening before plunging into the dark wastes of forest behind them, receiving from Uncle Tom their last supplies of flour, bacon, and tea. (Since coffee had to be ground, this was seldom included; Besides, tea was the traditional fare of the wilderness since Hudson Bay days.)

Uncle Tom's do-it-yourself hospital did not have large numbers of patients, but it was known that the Indian chief, Busticogan, dispensed medicine there on occasion, once brewing a tea of willow leaves as a pain reliever, and a sedative for a nervous settler's wife from some mysterious herbs.

It was also an impromptu dentist office. A lumberjack might be taken to a bigger town for treatment of a broken leg or smashed skull, but an aching tooth—never. Uncle Tom himself once submitted to such an operation, and lived to tell about it. Indians were visiting at a time when he was bedevilled by an aching tooth. It seemed only natural that Busticogan should pull it for him. But Uncle Tom wanted to be brave for the ordeal, so he dosed himself liberally with his home brew for an anesthetic. Busticogan apparently wanted to be brave, too, and kept pace with Uncle Tom. Eventually they felt ready for the operation, and Busticogan seized the offending tooth with the pliers. But Uncle Tom wasn't as near unconscious as he had wanted to be. The interested spectators were treated to the sight of Uncle Tom and Busticogan both dancing about clinging to the pliers, with Busticogan uttering encouraging grunts and Uncle Tom making the sounds of a moose in labor. Merciful friends intervened, and Uncle Tom was hauled ignominiously to a Grand Rapids dentist with his mouth hanging open, the tooth half in and half out.

At no time in the north country was a traveler ever denied food and lodging, either in the camps or at Uncle Tom's. Whether there was work for him or not, he was welcome to eat his fill and make use of a bunk, and no questions asked unless it appeared he intended to make an extended stay. The food was not such as could tempt a traveler to stay needlessly, being mostly such staples as beans and moose stew, as has been said. Uncle Tom was believed to have varied the fare at his establishment in a somewhat imaginative manner, according to the testimony of Jim Reid. He, with his partners Hawkins and Blake, dined royally at Uncle Tom's, eating the best stew they had enjoyed in many a day. Enjoyed, that is, until Uncle Tom disclosed the recipe—it was muskrat. Jim claimed that he managed to retain his share, but that the other two had to retire to the rear of the cabin.

Moose was readily available, and Uncle Tom frequently supplied the camps, from his excellent hunting site. Once he spotted one at some distance from his cabin, shot it, and paddled out in his canoe to get it. But the moose was not killed, merely stunned, and was understandably annoyed. It charged the canoe. Uncle Tom reversed direction at top speed and paddled furiously for safety, shouting over his shoulder at the irate animal, "You let me alone, I let you alone!"

Whatever the menu, Uncle Tom's wares were popular. It is not known whether he had guests the evening he was seen walking homeward with a brace of blackbirds in hand, muttering, "Chickanne, chickanne, alla time chickanne." His liquid refreshments were known to be potent medicine. Once he gave himself an accidental overdose, and in trying to light his pipe, burned off his beard. But Uncle Tom has dignity as a figure of history. He was the link between the era of logging and the era of settlement. He was the first settler-logger.

The forests have known many faces. We have the voyageurs and couriers-de-bois, followed by the canthook loggers and timber pirates, with the legitimate loggers and their axe-men coming last.

But were the voyageurs really first? I've wondered about it, especially since hearing an experience of P.C. Warner.

Percy Warner was Itasca County Surveyor for a long time. His services were invaluable, at a time when there were many problems concerning land and timber rights. His accuracy was proverbial, and his honesty and integrity were unquestionable. So, when he told me this

Buzzing down a beauty the old way. Two good men with a crosscut saw could do the job in ten minutes. (Ben Rajala col.)

story, I never had a moment's doubt as to its truth. It's the explanation that I find baffling.

As a young man in the 1890's, he was working with an old surveyor, running a line along the shores of Cass Lake. He was cutting line when he saw on a steep bank a black object, wrapped in a long birch roll. Curious, he tried to rake it down with a long pole. But the old surveyor objected. He growled, "Don't tamper with anything here. This is sacred burial ground."

Warner went on about his work, but he couldn't forget what he had seen, and during his lunch period he returned to the place, working at the thing until he got it.

It was a sword, six feet long, with the hilt or grip long enough to contain both his hands. The material was dark, shiny steel, without a speck of rust, and the blade was still sharp. To swing it required the strength of both of his hands. He was excited—it had to be of antique, historic value. He brought it with him, and dragged it along as he chopped the line, in spite of the angry muttering of the old surveyor.

When they came to a corner, suddenly the old surveyor changed his course, turning a perpendicular angle. This entailed cutting into the heavy brush and timber, and left Warner no choice but to leave the sword behind until they returned in the evening. He stuck it up in the sand near the corner, where he could locate it easily, and went on cutting line.

The old surveyor prevented his return in the evening by taking another diagonal through the woods toward camp, while allowing Warner to believe they would return to work there the next day. But that never happened. For the rest of the week they moved to a distant area, working long hours with no time to return. Then they left the area for another project across the lake.

Warner said he always wanted to return, but never had, and invited me to go along to hunt for the sword. We planned the trip. Soon after, he died. I've often longed to go there and search, but have never done so. Perhaps the sword is still there.

Where did the sword come from? What strong man wielded it? No one ever doubted P.C. Warner's veracity. Will we ever know the answer?

ONE-MAN SAW

TUTTLE TOOTH

2

The Trailblazers

Paul logged in other places besides Minnesota. When he logged off North and South Dakota, there was all them stumps left standing. But Paul took care of that. He had Big Ole the Blacksmith make him a maul, and he beat them stumps down into the ground, so now Dakota is mostly flat, without any trees.

There were such men as Black Jack Wilson, John (Canada Jack) Molan, Big Ike, Johnny Burdells, Art Sanborn, Joe Poquette, John Nelson. Strong-minded men, with equally strong, tough physiques. They were lean, leathery, grizzled stalwarts for the most part, far into their seventies mostly, when I knew them, with good health and longevity which might be attributed to their life of walking.

They were men with similar traits, different from the common lot. As a general rule, they were loners. Relying on basic principles of truth, honesty, hard work, determination, and persistence made them much alike, while, in a sense, a league apart from others.

These were the cruisers, the men on whom, more than anybody else, depended the success of the logging company's operations. They were the scouts, the vanguard of the full-scale war on the timber that came after. It was their job to go off into the wilderness, walk where no other white man had walked, and "cruise" the land: find the timber, estimate how much there was, what kind, how sound, what chances for roads, which streams. They kept maps and charts that showed swamps, ravines, cliffs—anything that might enter into the company's calculations in figuring out the job.

I learned a lot from them, though none were highly-educated in academic terms. They were self-taught men, very exacting in figures and facts. They had a great sense of humor; of Molan, they said he could "live on snow, if necessary, or the bark of trees, or hard tack, if he had a little tea."

This was said in admiration. The old cruisers were often too far from camps to pack food supplies other than flour, beans, bacon, and tea. Most of the time they foraged for themselves. Moose, deer, partridge, fish, rabbit, woodchuck, berries, cattails, water lily root stocks, wild onions, mushrooms, and herbs were all staples of their diet.

A cruiser's working method was simple—he walked the land, his far-ranging eyes sweeping the terrain as he covered each tally. The tally, as applied to timber cruising, was 330 feet, one-fourth of a quarter-mile. For working purposes, a quarter-mile (1,320 feet) was the average distance of one side of a 40-acre tract. However, when townships are divided into sections and subdivided into forties, the measurement varies greatly from this figure.

The average man, walking, took a thirty-inch step or "pace," and easily developed the habit of counting paces: 133 paces to a tally. More often, they used the double pace—counting every second step, which made sixty-six-and-one-half double-paces in a tally of 330 feet. The cruiser would stop every hundred feet, or more frequently in denser timber, taking a count of the average trees and species in his range of vision, an acre of area, jotting down the information in his notebook. The cruiser had to have an eagle eye, to know what he saw, and judge all the variables.

After covering the distance of one tally, a "tally-whack" axe-mark was blazed on a tree. These were numbered consecutively: Tally 1, Tally 2, 3, and 4. Using this method, the cruiser recorded not only the timber, but pertinent information regarding the land, the water courses, swamps, or hills encountered. From this data was compiled total volumes of timber on a particular description of land, as well as a land map important in laying out a logging plan.

The old method of timber cruising included "horseshoeing," or making a cruise to estimate the timber inside the forty. This entailed walking the land in a U or horseshoe pattern one tally in from the lines. Of course this resulted in more accurate findings.

Nowadays there are much more sophisticated techniques. Modern foresters use aerial maps, stereoscopes, and computers, doing it all right in the comfort of the office chair.

Besides the old Jacobs compass, the land surveyors used a chain for accuracy in land measurement. The chain had 100 links and was a total of sixty-six feet in length. Five chains equalled one tally, eighty chains a mile. The crudeness of the equipment didn't prevent their doing an amazingly precise job.

John Nelson had grown up in the timber and cruising. He had an easy smile, and I never knew him to be less than good-natured. Like Wilson, his predecessor, he was "in the know." The cruiser's was a position of trust, and few were chosen for it. Nelson's training and abilities were well-tailored to handle the raucous problems of the gyppo logging contractors, and these were considerable. The turmoil that developed among these contractors, fighting for position, was fierce.

The M & O Company, the reorganization of Backus' companies after his death, required the cool judgment of a man like Nelson. Though the problems of timber and lands were easily settled in his jurisdiction, he might have a quiet word of discipline on road rights, or some similar bone of contention, among the competing contractors. They all respected his authority, and everyone liked him.

Art Sanborn was another of the same school of men, trusted with high responsibility. He spoke with vast and comprehensive knowledge regarding timber and logging. When he visited the camp, you somehow wanted to do your best in response to the advice and inspiration he gave.

Johnny Burdelle was more sturdily built, yet he got through the woods very nimbly, locating corners. All of a sudden he would appear out of nowhere, silent as a shadow. I sometimes wondered if he had inherited his ability to move without sound from his French-Indian ancestors, along with his dark eyes and black hair. His speech, too, was quiet and brief, and he seemed mostly lost in his own deep thoughts. It was said that his cruise estimates were always "on the money," the highest accolade for accuracy.

Joe Poquette was a peppery Frenchman, who, they said, had done everything an all-around lumberjack ever did: cut pine, drive logs, top load, and occasionally "jump astraddle of a cookstove and run off a batch of sourdough flapjacks as good as the best of 'em." He liked to tell of all the log drives he had taken down the river. When I met him, he was back in the woods, hacking lines and trails to "let the daylight in," so we could see how to get the last of the pine out. He was good at all kinds of jobs, but not long on patience. The racket the cats and trucks made really raised his blood pressure—he would curse a blue streak at them, using words I'd never heard before or since.

Big Ike had no other name, that I recall. He was tall, and long of leg, reminding you of a crane, walking with a three foot even stride that was born of tallying miles of section lines and driving stakes. His foot action was springy as he stepped over windfalls or stumps. His long arms swung the axe easily, and brush and trees always seemed to fall clear of the line. When he spoke, it was in a humorous vein, in a deep growl, making some remark about the "forty line getting too long." But his pace count and direction were uncannily accurate. When he had traveled 440 paces, you could depend on an old corner post being near his last pace.

The most romantic figure was BlackJack Wilson. He was a tall, slender man, quick of step, with dark piercing eyes that seemed to take in all the surroundings at a glance. He had a dark and graying beard, and spoke in quiet, commanding tones with something of a "Down-easter" accent. Occasionally we saw him going east, in the dead of cold winter, with a pack sack and a pair of snow shoes on his shoulder. The area he traveled was twenty to thirty miles of uninhabited forest wilderness. It might be three weeks or more before we saw him return, and we often wondered where he stayed, and what he lived on in the starvation-time of winter. My father told us he built a thick lean-to of tree boughs and a good fire.

His job was cruising the country, ahead of logging and railroad routing. On one occasion before 1925, he stopped at our house for lunch, and in the discussion mentioned that at the rate railroad logging was advancing through the area, the pine timber would last only ten years more.

STUMP, SHOWING UNDERCUT,
AND LOG

I believe Wilson had a special respect for my father, coupled with liking and trust, which eventually led to our family's involvement in extensive logging contracts. Once my father reminisced of something that had happened long before, in 1915, when he had spent the winter in one of Backus' camps. He came home in the spring, only to be shocked at the discovery that Backus' loggers had cut about twenty-five pine trees over the line, on his land. This was serious. It was the only green timber that had been left to him—fire had swept the homestead nearly clear of standing timber. Naturally he prized it highly, and it was the cornerstone of his plans for future building. Now he had no possibility of lumber from any source.

He brought this to Wilson's attention. Wilson counted the stumps. With no further ado, he said, "Ivar, we'll get you some timber and make it right."

He was as good as his word. For years after that, Father often got odd forties of scattered pine or cedar, and other timber, to clean up at some bargain. The trespass was paid for many times over.

I remember Wilson stopping to see my father another time, and telling him, "There has been some trespass, approximately a hundred thousand board feet, on Section 28 near Deer Lake. I'd like t'have you take a look at it, then take the contract to skid and haul it to the railroad landing near Thistledew Camp."

Father and my older brothers did take the job. The irony of it was, the truckers they hired to haul the timber were laughing slyly the whole time. It was obvious they knew all too well who were the trespassers.

It was said no man knew more about the timber in the Littlefork and Big Fork Valleys than BlackJack Wilson. He had been to every section that contained valuable stands of pine, cedar, and spruce; had seen with his own eyes vast, beautiful stands of virgin timber; jotted down notes in his logbook which were no doubt, used in the formulating and founding of E. W. Backus' lumbering empire.

He was a rare man, absolute in judgment, resolute in purpose. His word was his bond. Though his days were filled with dutiful tasks, there was no doubt he spent time deliberating in clear thoughts, reflecting on matters of profound importance, sitting alone at his evening campfire. Lacking all social amenities, he felt the inadequacy. Nevertheless, he had a deep sense of oneness with nature, and felt at home in the company of trees.

Wilson was E. W. Backus' head cruiser. As it happened, the depression hit full force on Backus' far-flung operations. At the same time, Backus died. This brought to an end any further railroad building into the area that is now the George Washington State Forest of Minnesota. From that time, the logging was done by "gyppo" or contract loggers, and company cruisers roamed the woods no more.

Almost to a man, cruisers were sincere and upright in their dealings. The companies relied on them absolutely, and the cruisers gave selflessly and without stinting, with well-deserved pride in their calling. They had other dangers to contend with besides being wet or cold or hungry, or threatened by wild animals. There was an ever-present threat of spies who would stop at nothing to seize their precious logbooks. Art Matthieu told me about a cruiser for Matthieu Lumber Company who failed to report after a reasonable time, was searched for, and was found, shot dead. His bag and all his cruising estimates were gone. It was a grim, bitter price to pay for doing a job.

Holding, as they did, the key to logging bonanzas, it speaks well for these men that they weren't constantly using this knowledge for their own advantage. However, one man who worked all winter for a large logging company kept his findings in two sets of books. He cruised in such a way as to keep the timber land in a long running block, keeping a separate private record of especially choice stands. When his work was done, he turned in his company books with his cruising records of ordinary timber, bringing them to the company's office. He knew well that these would be studied carefully for some time, before any action was taken, or efforts made to file claims. That gave him plenty of time to make his way to the land office, where he proceeded to file his own claims to the choice timberland. From there he high-tailed it to New York, where he made a proposal to some friendly financiers. He returned with the wherewithal to build a railroad and run a sizeable logging operation on the lands he'd cruised at his company's expense.

There were even a few cruisers who weren't so phenomenally accurate. It's been told that one who estimated timber elsewhere in Minnesota surveyed the Rum River watershed and stated flatly that the timber would last for seventy years. His estimate was long—he missed by about sixty years!

Cruisers had certain authority from their companies, but seldom were sticklers over minor matters. When Black Jack Wilson and his compass man, Charley Sprague, found where Frank Werthner had logged windfall timber a wee bit over the line, helping himself to a small amount of Backus' timber, they said off-handedly that it was a good thing Frank had cleaned it up and kept it from being a fire hazard. Frank's neighbor was not so lucky. When he cut some cedar ties that happened to be on State land, two State cruise scalers raised a fuss, making him pay double stumpage for the trespass. Such rigorous penalty against a small homesteader seems rather unfair, in the light of whole townships of timber having been stolen by big outfits who got away scot-free.

Jack Molan, medium build and size, walked with an easy stride and 30" pace, stopping every 40 paces to write down the tally. It was a marvel how he took accurate count of all merchantable-size trees of various species. When total production scales were completed, his cruising estimates were surprisingly in balance with timber production.

He had worked as head cruiser on the logging railroad layout for Frank Gillmor of Virginia Rainy Lake Lumber Company's operations, during the time of their logging north of Virginia, Minnesota.

He never seemed to miss the corner post. When he'd gone the prescribed number of paces, if the cornerpost had been destroyed by decay or fire, and was gone, he'd dig a little with his axe, and there it would be—the original corner stake, under leaf mold, showing definitely the axe work of the original surveyor nearly sixty years earlier.

He had a quick, agile, mathematical mind, and could devise an engineering formula for almost anything. When he was a little "hard-oiled" he liked to pass these gems of wisdom on. Once he told me, in his rasping Irish brogue, "Kid, for our purposes, all forties are square. To get the hypotenuse, you can take a right triangle on the side of a forty, 1,320 feet, and multiply by 1.425 and so many other little things." He was a master of lightning calculation, coming up with an answer to a long mathematical problem without ever resorting to a pencil. His formula for finding distances along a right triangle involved reducing the three sides to some multiples of three, four, and five. Long before "Modern Math" was heard of, he was using its principles in rapid mental gyrations that left most observers bewildered.

Molan said that many times when his compass broke down, or mineral attraction was too strong for a compass to be dependable, he would improvise by using his watch. By placing it with the hour hand pointing to the sun, and twelve o'clock to the north, he was able to continue working in any direction. He even went one step further when both the compass and the watch went "kerflooie"—he estimated the sun's height and angle for the hour of the day, then sighted the direction from time to time from the shadow of his forefinger.

CRUISER'S AXE,
PACK AND COMPASS

One of his fancies was a "high stump car" he pretended he was going to build—he said he was worn out in late years from all the cars he'd pushed out of mudholes on backwoods roads, not from walking the 550,000 miles he'd paced off on section lines in his time. This car had most elaborate plans. It would have two engines, two transmissions, two radiators, two gas tanks, two batteries, so there would always be a spare in case of breakdown. It would have lots of high wheels, and tires with built-in chains so it would never get stuck, or break down completely. This, he said, would solve all motoring problems that we all struggled with on the back roads of the time.

Molan liked to work with brother Sam on the bulldozer, blazing logging trails ahead of the cat. "Sam can get that monster through the woods like a weasel, while doing the work of a crew of giants," he'd say. He was filled with admiration for the big juggernauts, telling us, "They're a real savior of cruisers' legs in one sense, with a nice, smooth road to walk back on. But the hard thing is, I can't run fast enough to keep ahead."

Once a month, on a certain date, he would come to me: "I'd like t'wheel me inta town, gotta take care of m' eastern mail." I'd take him to town for his pension check. His next stop would be the "hard oil station." Three or four days later he'd come dragging back to camp, badly bent out of shape. After a rest and some chuck he'd be ready to go again: "Gotta get back to work, finish cruising."

Restless-footed, he had surveyed all the way to Hudson Bay, and walked back to Duluth. He'd surveyed along the Canadian boundary from Lake Superior to Rainy Lake; worked along the Mississippi River dikes to the Gulf of Mexico; and retraced the Mason-Dixon Line. He'd spent years with the Canadian railroad survey, charting miles of bridges and trestles. All these adventures he told of, sitting with cup in hand by the lunchtime campfire. Then, finishing his tea and rising from the log, he'd say he'd "just love to see the other side of this 40" or section we were cruising, total the figures, and "get some action going." He was late into his seventies at the time; he lived until after World War II.

I never saw him after I went away to the war in 1942, but often I wish I had. Perhaps we'll meet some day at the campfire in the Big Pine Woods, where all good loggers go.

SNOWSHOES

✑ 3 ✑

The Settler-Loggers

Loggin' wasn't always easy for Paul. There was one stand on a pine hill so thick that when they cut all the trees on one side of the hill, the hill fell over because of the weight of the trees on the other side. One rainy year the trees grew so fast Paul's seven axemen just couldn't keep up with it. They'd hit the tree one swipe with the axe, and by then it would have grown so much they couldn't reach to hit it again in the same cut.

The old order persisted, with the big companies operating large camps well into the 1930s. But a new era had grown beside it. The men who lived in the region were taking over the job of logging off what was left after the Timber Barons packed their turkeys and left for the West Coast.

"Timber Barons" has become a dirty word, but it's time to recognize that their operations had some good aspects, too. They opened the country, by providing roads and trails, and railroads. They brought in potential settlers and when the immigrants began to outnumber the shanty-boys in the camps, the old roistering days, when everything was war either against the forces of nature or fellow timber-beasts, were numbered. And when these men took homesteads, the camp provided them with a livelihood. Not only could they sell their produce to the camps—which always needed potatoes and hay—but they could put their teams to work in winter, skidding, or they could go to cutting. Most farmers wore two hats at the time, as a matter of course. In summer, when the camps were idle, they cleared and brushed and planted and built (sometimes with supplies from the camp, which kept the land-clearing jobs supplied with dynamite). Freeze-up would find them back in their woolen mackinaws and stag pants, spending nights in the bunkhouse with the rest of the jacks. If a logging job was close to home, a man might stay there, but the extra travel was just that much more hard labor, and most of them went into the woods in the fall and came out only for visits until the job was done.

In one case, at least, the homesteaders made good use of the lumber camps' hospitality—the first settlers in the area in the 1890s lived in a vacant Loper and Rumery camp. And anyone could stop in for a meal at any time, with no questions asked.

There was a little more control of the timber after Koochiching County became an entity separate from Itasca in 1906. Previous to that, the area was so large as to be unmanageable from an administrator's point of view. There was no telling who was cutting where in the back-woods.

There was still plenty of big pine. Orin Patrow thought the prime stand was in Section 19 of Township 62, Range 24. The logs from here were easy to identify on the drive, even when mingled with other logs. Not only did they have a regular stamp-hammer brand, but a big boulder jutting out into Deer Creek left a special imprint when the logs hit it, The large stumps still visible testify to the truth of Orin's judgment.

The Titanic Camp, a 200-man operation run by Sandy McClellan, was huge even by the standards of the time. It ran two shifts, with head-lights on the horses for night loading and hauling. Spike Patrow claimed that they had three crews—one coming, one going, and one working. Operated by Conner Brothers on a Red River Lumber Company lease, they took out the biggest cork pine some of the old timers ever remem-bered, averaging two-and-a-half logs per thousand board feet.

The loads were huge—cork pine being light, the loaders could pile on all they wanted, 12,000 to 15,000 board feet to a four-horse sleigh. On a drive, the logs were buoyant, floating like the corks they were called. Three or four million board feet were taken out in each of the two years the camp operated, 1910 to 1912.

A Namakan camp in the Bowstring area housed 160 men in the years from 1908 to 1911. Many of the crew were homesteaders who lived near by. Duncan Price was the woods superintendent, with many camps under his authority strung along the Big Fork River. The resident fore-man was Jim Hayes, who later was killed when a tree fell on a locomo-tive in which he was riding. Weyerhaeuser had a timber camp in the area, also, logged by Sam Simpson. These logs were hoisted on the Itasca Lumber Company Railroad at Dora Lake, and went south. (Oddly enough, after railroading, some of these logs were dumped in the Mis-sissippi for another long drive to Minneapolis mills.)

Throughout the history of the camps we keep hearing the names of men who left their mark on the area in other ways, like Charles Godfrey, whose father built two steam tugboats for booming logs across the lake, which Charley operated. Eventually Charley became County Land Commissioner.

Even though the old ways worked well, the companies weren't opposed to new ideas. Namakan tried two steam-powered "high-lead skidders," a system developed in Michigan which became highly specialized in the mountain logging of the West. By rigging up cables to tall spar trees, and using cable chokers, they were able to move tree-length timber out easily. But the U.S. Forest Service objected—they said it damaged the young second growth. Perhaps it did, but in any case Namakan moved the skidders to Canada and used them there.

Skelly Brothers, logging south of the Divide, used a steam donkey winch to get out timber in rough country where the hills were too steep for horses. They loaded sleighs in the the bottoms of the ravines and hollows with no outlets, then winched the loads up to where the horses could take over.

Summer logging presented skidding problems, but Stitt and Company figured out a way to get timber to water even then. They laid down a pair of long skids like railroad tracks, leading to the creek a half-mile away, and greased them. Logs were chained together, fifteen or so in a group, with a horse hitched at each end, and down to the water they went. There was one problem. The teamster, Emil Kyllonen, had trouble finding enough grease for the operation—he was using up the bacon and salt pork rinds faster than the camp could provide them.

The "grab it and git" boys hadn't left the country before the new breed took hold—the settler loggers.

The dean of the corps has to be Leonard Dickinson, and he certainly points up the difference. Anyone who has seen Hollywood's stereotype of a lumberjack—noisy, brawling, with a strong back and a weak mind— would never guess him to be one. He looks and sounds like an ex-senator (which he is): courtly, witty, and articulate. But he's also the man who's shipped timber to the Northwest Paper Company of Cloquet the longest of any of their suppliers: seventy years.

He has a couple of other firsts: first white child born at Buena Vista, and first birth recorded in Turtle Lake township. He watched the old give place to the new in many ways: the old Indian trails becoming roads, and the old fur post falling into decay. How the post was built was a mystery—it was a frame building, but no one knew where the lumber had come from, whether whipsawed on the site or carried in. Their family saga is loaded with pioneer history. His grandfather probably holds the world's record for building homestead shacks, having made his in an hour and twenty minutes.

Settlers always needed money, and logging was the obvious way to get it. Leonard learned logging from his father. "Most outfits of the time used oxen, mostly because everybody else did, but we didn't use them." Leonard says. The coming of the railroad was a memorable event. Rails and rolling stock had to be freighted in, a mammoth undertaking. The long string of twelve teams which hauled in the locomotive, with teamster Paul Fournier driving, made an unforgettable sight. Shallow lakes had to be corduroyed to prevent the enormous load from breaking through the ice, and swamp roads had to be corduroyed, too.

He got his feet wet in the business when he purchased and logged his grandfather's timber, and then his father's, and followed it up by working as a toploader for the railroad.

One season, he logged for Molander of the Red Lake Railroad Company. Molander was pessimistic, having been stung before in the chancy logging business, but he wanted his timber out. "But don't come around next spring saying I owe you money," he warned. Leonard went to work, with $600 capital furnished by his parner. Evidently Molander didn't have high expectations, because when his young partner came to settle up at the end of the season, Molander wasn't at all pleased to see him. He nearly swallowed his Adam's apple when Leonard reported a profit of $1,600 on the deal, and gave him a check. For once in his life, he'd come out in the black. As for Leonard, he was now launched as a logger.

Logging for the railroad meant supplying ties. These were mostly hewed by hand, with a broad axe. A tiemaker was a person of some skill. It was said of one man that he could hew along a string guide and never disturb it.

In this period of rapid expansion, ties were a big item. Dickinson furnished all the ties for the Red Lake railroad, and eventually had one of the first contracts with Great Northern, for 10,000 ties. I doubt if there is another logger living with more "firsts" to his credit.

In the Big Fork Valley, the magic name was Orin Patrow. The country would never have been the same without him. As has been said, he began logging for the big companies: Namakan, which replaced Keewatin in the organization, and Putnam. It was through Dunc Price that he got started on his own. The superintendent told him of seven forties which he had tried to buy for Namakan without success; but, he thought, if Orin would try, there was a good chance he could get it. And Namakan would stake him to his logging outfit, including camp, horses, sleighs.

This was an offer Orin couldn't refuse. The $5,800 advance was a staggering burden, but Orin was by now a married man (having successfully courted the Valley's schoolma'am), and he was never a man to duck a thing because it was risky. Price had picked his man well—Orin was a go-getter, a tireless dynamo of a man who would have turned night into day if he could. He told his crew no man needed a watch on his jobs: when you could see the stars, and no earlier, it was time to quit.

The new enterprise was a booming success. From this beginning, he continued to log for Namakan. Lands with more than fifteen thousand feet of standing pine timber per forty were not allowable homesteads, but were retained by the state until logged. The pine from these areas had to be cut so the land could be opened for the clamoring settlers. Time was a big factor—waste and slashings had to be disposed of right now, and fire was the only applicable method. It was debatable whether this was more good than bad. Certainly it was more harmful to young trees, and sometimes the fires escaped their bounds, but by some strange alchemy of nature, the heat of the fire helped regenerate new stands.

Between logging jobs, Orin cleared his own land and started farming. He tried to bring his logging know-how to bear on the problem of removing stumps, but had to give up winching them out with a jammer. It was too tough, with too much soil clinging to the massive root system. In his (so-called) spare time, Orin located claims for would-be settlers. One of these was a city-bred damsel whose fancy outfit was more suited to teapartying than roughing it. In desperation, Orin hauled her piggyback part of the distance—and was rewarded by being immortalized in her book about the adventure, "The Cloth Wagon."

BROAD AXE

Thereafter he scouted out logging jobs of his own, cutting the timber on his own place and buying stumpage from neighbors.

On one occasion he hauled a U.S. Postal Inspector from Big Fork, down river to Ripple (which was later named Big Falls), and finally on to Emo, Ontario. There he sold the boat for five dollars, and started to make the return trip on foot. It was a grueling hike, wallowing through swamps and beset with mosquitoes. The only short cut was afforded when Ross Slack, homesteading at Riley Brook, showed him from a high ridge how to cut off the winding river oxbow. Eventually he reached Kinney trail, cut by an early homesteader to appease his lonesome wife, and got to Big Fork. The hundred-mile trip took him four days.

Community matters and other business slowed his logging activity, but in 1923-24 he went "one more"—a big white and Norway pine job for Haywire O'Connell, near Deer Lake. The whole crew was local men. Orin's brother Spike was cook, Tom and Gunder Gunderson (two strapping, powerful axemen), the Harrington boys, and others cut the last of the big stands. My father, Ivar Rajala, with his brother Frank Peterson, hauled logs with four-horse teams to the high bank landings along the Big Fork. It was the last big sleigh-haul to the river, bringing to an end the era of old-style pine operations. It was also the first time I ever saw the falling and loading of big pines.

We were filled with excitement when, on Saturdays, we could hitch our sleds behind the big loaded sleighs and ride to the river. We'd watch speechless with tension as the chains were tripped, and the logs cascaded in a tumbling mass down on the river. I could hardly contain my anticipation when I was considered old enough to go along on a trip to the camp. The distance seemed endless, though only three or four miles, winding among old cutover stumps, passing through the snow-covered wonderland of trees where small thickets of spruce or balsam glittered like Christmas trees, with scattered lone pines standing out like sentinels guarding the dark timber line in the distance. The birds and rabbits seemed just as excited as I was.

We passed the old Camp 5 buildings, or what was left of them, now mostly rotten or burned down. Only the remaining base logs and snow-covered dirt embankments were visible. The old ruins had somehow an aura of great events long past.

Finally we reached the new camps, covered with tarpaper and slabs, with smoke swirling up and away in the breeze, and pines standing all around.

Spike, the cook, seemed surrounded by magical equipment—the big black wood-burning cookstove with steaming kettles, the shiny tin cups and plates on the long tables, and the variety of heavy utensils: ladles, dippers, cleavers, butcher knives, all larger than I'd ever seen, hanging from a board above the big cupboard. Every detail, including the sun streaming through the skylight, caused great wonderment in me.

He was working at the big baking board, making great loaves of bread. It seemed part of a dream when he offered us raisin pie and doughnuts and coffee. Seemingly he knew how I felt: he smiled and chuckled, and spoke of how I was no doubt a good boy, somehow reminding me of Santa Claus. I felt that somehow he was very great, larger than life.

Then we followed the logging road to where logs were being loaded in the sleighs. Modern log loading seems insignificant by comparison now. Yet I've always enjoyed the exciting spirit that is a part of it. There always remains the same awesome sensation when you see big logs in action.

As it was then, the toploader picking and calling for the next log to come rolling up the skids, the skidway man "cutting" the log to keep it straight, the top loader calling "Whoa!" and the crosshaul team stopping, remains a picture in my mind. The loader knocked out the hook and called "Chain!"; the crosshaul team responded, trotting back. The next log was wrapped, and the toploader set the hook again with a heavy sledge. Around and around they seemed to go, with the log load built up to a scary height, probably twelve feet high and twelve feet wide. Corner binds were put on, wrapper chains laid, and a binding pole twisted tightly in the chains, securing the logs.

Starting the big sleighs was equally exciting, as they swung the big teams into place and hitched up. The teams were swung to the side. Then the teamster spoke firmly to the horses and they seemed to crouch down, straining their great muscles. The whole thing seemed as if bound to the ground, unable to move. Finally it eased forward all at once, and started, slowly, screeching against the snow. As it gained speed, it appeared majestic in movement, something that called for triumphant music.

Then we watched and marveled at the felling of the great dark white pines and the tall reddish-barked Norway, with their long, clean trunks and bushy tops that appeared to reach the sky. Somehow we already knew the difference between the trees from my father's talk.

We were warned to stay clear from the areas of falling trees, and I'm sure the excitement and dangerously-loud sounds kept me at the safely prescribed distance. But the older brothers soon found some high stumps that we could climb on. From these vantage points we could see the fallers bent over their crosscut saws, with streams of sawdust flying past their legs as they pulled, and hear the singing buzz of the saw; and the swampers, with many axes chopping. The ringing of hammering and wedges echoed everywhere. We would see the faint motion as the wide crown of the tree started to sway, hear the voices of the fallers, Big Tom and Gunder, calling out their signal, "Timm-BERRR!," warning everybody to get clear.

I held my breath as with first a whispering and then a singing of pine needles, and a whistling, the majestic giants gained speed, and came thundering and crashing to the ground, with echoes booming and trailing away off into the woods. Then all was silent and still as glistening clouds of silvery snow rose from its resting place, then drifted gently back to earth.

With such a beginning, no wonder logging has always held a fascination for me.

Still another man who came to log and stayed to settle was Frank Werthner. He was a free-lancer who put in time at various company camps. His first job for Namakan might well have been his last, for he worked under a cross-eyed foreman, Stewart Fraser, whose orders were not aimed at the men he meant them for. Frank was put with a gang of outlanders to do brushing. Everything under three inches was at that time piled and burned. The job wasn't hard, and Frank flew into it, though his fellow workers, once the boss had disappeared, spent most of their time cozily chatting around the fire.

In time Fraser came to check on their progress, and was more than a little displeased. He fixed Frank with his wandering eye and informed him it was a lousy showing: "You got to do better than that!" Frank's blood boiled. He felt he had done a good bit more than his share, and here he was the one who got bawled out. Simmering over the unjust accusation, he decided to quit; it was nearly Christmas, anyway. He marched up to the office, turned in his axe, and asked for his time.

TWO-MAN CROSSCUT SAW
AND AXE

Fraser arrived right on his heels, and was dismayed at Frank's reaction. "But I wasn't talking to you!" he said. But Frank, having made up his mind, refused to stay. He started for Bigfork, fourteen miles away, and two hours and fifteen minutes later was drowning his irritation in the first of its seven saloons.

A versatile man, Frank worked at a number of different jobs. Repairing the dams on Deer Creek was one, replacing apron planks and chute, and making gates. The gate at Lower Dam was a half-moon, with a rubber belt, and raised and lowered sidewise by a windlass. Water pressure, half on the gate and half on the wall, held the belt. Some timbers in the dams themselves and the gate had to be replaced, and rocks and dirt that had washed out refilled.

Another job was cutting hay for the camp horses, in the summers. This took a three-man gang, cutting hay with scythes one day, raking and shocking it the next, and finally picking up the shocks by sliding two slender peeled spruce poles under the shock and lifting them to carry the shock to the stack. For this they were paid eight dollars a ton, and their efforts usually produced about that much, or perhaps more, in a day. It was not coarse wild grass but blue-joint and red-top, of good quality. Where horses had seeded some areas along roads from their droppings, there was even timothy, and clover.

Building camps was another chore. Here again, Frank seemed fated to fall in with malingerers. Men who worked with him at a camp at Twin Creek south of Pickerel Lake on Quinn's meadows walked four miles each way to the job. The hike took so long, what with their frequent pauses to rest, that slow walkers could only work a couple of hours before it was time to start back.

As a year-round resident, he got involved in other activity. When sawmills came into the country, the camps began to be built of lumber. Backus' camp at Bass Lake in 1913 was of this construction. When the job was over, Frank Smith, the former camp cook, had his eye on the material for his own purposes. He got together a salvage crew consisting of himself, Tom Brady, and Frank Werthner. Together they dismantled the buildings; so far, so good. But coming back with their load was another matter. The ice on spring-fed Bass Lake was "rotten." Werthner was persuaded to walk ahead of the team to detect unsafe spots, while Brady drove, both alert to the slightest sign of danger. They were well on their way when Frank felt the ice begin to give way, and shouted a warning. In the nick of time Brady swung the team back to shore, missing drowning them by a whisker.

More and more, the men of the camps were a part of the community. Jess Bowerman, Tom Brady, Walt McCorkell, and Frank Werthner, all bachelors, spent considerable time scouting around the country on personal activities, looking for good trapping spots and berry patches. Bog cranberries are extinct in the region now, but they found a bog where each of them picked a bushel, with plenty left over for the bears.

Not having families, they sort of became "Dutch Uncles" to all the neighborhood boys. One year, as a special treat they pooled their resources for an oyster feed. Jess Bowerman put up fifty dollars for expenses, Frank collected the supplies, and Tom did the cooking. It was held in the school house, and was a highly festive occasion, with violin and accordion music, dancing, and presents for the children. I have never forgotten being carried there in my father's arms under the crisp cold winter starlight, while my mother carried my younger brother.

There were many homesteader-loggers, and I don't pretend that I knew them all, or will mention them all here. Everyone I ever knew was interesting to me.

Jim Reid wasn't slated for a logging career. He started as a school-master in New Brunswick. Infected with the urge to go west, he wound up in Bemidji in about 1898, where his skill with figures soon got him a job as bookkeeper. But this, he found, was a rather elastic designation. In reality he was a general factotum, even pressed into service to take down a drive. With all this experience behind him, he naturally went into the fascinating timber business for himself, supplying timber for the Backus company at Craig.

Lon Powell, Wick Powell, and Elmer Knotts all located along the Big Fork near Little Falls. Along with most of their neighbors, they had timber. Everybody followed the same procedure, logging it off to the river, where they sold the landed logs to Namakan, Backus, or Engler companies, for ten dollars and up per thousand feet. Knotts built up a business of supplying camps with beef and butter, while Powell, a man of serious mien and incredible strength, followed the timber.

Almost the first names to come to mind in any tale of the Valley are those of Godfrey and James Knight. Coming to the settlement as young lads, they reveled in the life, and became crackerjack woodsmen. It was quite natural that they would, coming from a long line of voyageur fur traders. Besides learning to rough it out in the wilderness and acquaint-ing themselves with all the lures that young lads were likely to encounter, Jim said their survival was best attributed to "being brought up on moose milk." Their humor added color and sparkle to the arduous life of the settler. Jim told all about his pioneering adventures in his witty book, "We Homesteaded."

At Effie, George Poole had a camp, with landings along the railroad nearly a mile long. Others supplied timber there: John Edstrom, Ed Opsahl, Nels Phillips. Mike and Len Rahier logged at Kenny Landing. Itasca Lumber Company, the logging arm of the Joyce and Pillsbury interests, had timber, with picked men doing the logging.

Practically every settler was involved one way or another. Andrew Anderson, O. T. Anenson, Halvor Aakhus, Frank and John Dahlberg, Gust Gustafson, William Welte—the list if complete would include the whole census. Andrew Anderson headed a group of his countrymen, Norwegians all, who functioned as a bloc. For some reason I could never figure out, their area was known as Sweden Valley.

Sid Williams had an operation going in 1923-1924 on the south bay of Larson Lake, just west of the narrows. Sid said he put two million feet of logs into the lake, mostly Norway pine. Some thirteen years later, Leonard Jensen and Gust Westvik pulled deadheads from the lake, but sawed only about 600,000 board feet from the venture. This would indicate that most of Sid's logs sank in deep water, and were never recovered.

Sid Williams was contract logging for Jack O'Connell, who was heard to complain bitterly that when a piece of equipment broke down, it was Sid's practice to swap it at O'Connell's headquarters camp for one that worked; the result was, according to his boss's lament, that at the end of the season, Sid had all good equipment and "Haywire" was left with feeble and defective sleighs, drays, harness and rigging.

Most loggers trusted the loyalty of their crews and were well able to do so, but at times a few rotten apples might get into the barrel. When Sid got suspicious of his cook and foreman (an old timer named George Scanlon) he prepared to test them out. He informed them that he would be gone for two or three days, and took his departure; but in reality he didn't go anywhere, and showed up on the job next day. His suspicions were justified: both men were drunk. Sid chased the cook down to the lake and threw him in. He then took out after Scanlon. Bystanders witnessed a chase like they'd never seen before and the two men covered a lot of ground at top (like a couple of low-flying rockets) speeds before Sid caught up with his foreman, and half-killed him before peacemakers intervened.

Somewhere in the same area as Sid's, near Bass Lake, Pris Peloquin had a logging camp, around 1912. We destroyed the remains of the old buildings when we set up a sawmill there. His younger brother Fred got his baptism of fire somewhat earlier, when the two of them were cutting logs as a team. Prisque was very skillful, and not one to put up with any body else's clumsiness. In making the last swing in the cut, the sawyer making the last slash had to make a quick judgment as to the amount of cutting through the final wood, and pull the saw upward as he finished, clear of the cut. Fred was new and understandably nervous, and missed his turn in the swing. Inevitably this pulled the saw toward his knee, and the downward pressure forced it into his leg. While they were wrapping the cut with a handkerchief (not much fancy first aid here), Prisque said unsympathetically, "Your own fault; serves you right." Fred said that never happened to him again.

Fred started in the woods as a mere stripling. Faced with the choice of either going back to school in southern Minnesota or going to work, he chose work, expecting that if he started on a job he would be able to quit later with little said. However, he soon found that he liked woods work, and never quit.

Since his elder brother Prisque was a respected woodsman of some standing, he had no trouble getting a job in the camp where his brother worked. The trouble was in the hours. The landing where the timber was picked up was some distance away. This made it necessary for the teamsters to make an early start, and breakfast was served to all hands at 4:30 A.M. This meant that the rank and file of the crew would then have an hour to kill before going out to work. Fred, as the pampered youngest son at home, found this a bitter tribulation. Brother Prisque solved it for him. Fred could go back to sleep after breakfast, and Prisque would wake him in time so that when the foreman opened the back door and walked the length of the bunkhouse, Fred would be ready with the others to follow him out the front door.

Fred's first assignment was to work with a man whom the boss pointed out to him. It was still too dark to see the man, but Fred could recognize him by the way he carried his axe, and followed him. Near the end of the trail the man stopped. Their job was to make a rollway at that spot, grubbing all trees and stumps, for a clean surface. Fred had spent the previous year clearing land, and along with the experience he had a burning desire to succeed. It wasn't too long before his partner warned him not to try to get the rollway completed in minutes, it was due to take them the entire day. When the foreman showed up to see how his new recruit was performing, his partner was able to recommend him.

The boss then brought him to another task. In the middle of the cut made for a road was a rock, too large to be moved by the horses. Fred's instructions were to build a hot fire in all sides of the rock, and keep it going until further notice. Fred went at this task with equal zeal, helped by the handy presence of some large dry tamarack. Presently the boss returned. This time he ordered Fred to pile snow on the rock, as rapidly as possible. It sounded odd, but the young man realized it was not for him to question the foreman, so he did as he was told. In moments he heard loud cracking as the rock split, and soon they could carry it off the road in pieces.

Thirty years after he'd left woods work, Fred came out to spend a day in the timber with me. He watched the modern logging activities for several hours, absorbed. Then he seemed to become impatient, and asked if I could get him a good axe, and a saw. We went to camp, had lunch, and found the necessary tools. Then he went to work on some big spruce grizzled with limbs, and I had a revelation. The axe work he did was amazing, as he chopped the big limbs with sure, even strokes, leaving a smooth, clean cut tree trunk. He had never lost his hard-won skill.

We often heard talk of the problems faced by loggers, and the way they met the challenges. There were many things that entered into the extremes of woods operations: timbered lands might be high, steep hills with ravines and rocky ledges, clay lowlands, or soggy swamps with floating bogs that must be traversed to reach the timber. The White, Norway, and jack pine of the high ground might be interspersed with aspen (popple), birch, or other brushy hardwoods. Clay lowlands might have white pine, spruce, balsam, and cedar, again mixed with popple and birch. Low swales likely contained ash and elm, whereas swampy lands grew black spruce and tamarack. All this was to be reckoned with, and practical means had to be devised to remove the timber. Without a reasonable appraisal of all economic pluses and minuses, it was easy to lose your shirt.

Finn George was to pass this test often enough to keep his shirt on, though it seemed he had more than his fair share of tough chances. One winter he had hills so steep he couldn't work horses on the slopes, and deep snow. No problem—he made slides in the snow, then iced them with water and let his logs go shooting down the hills. The timber was loaded on sleighs at the bottom of the ravines, and hauled out with very little sweat.

SAW FILE GAUGE

Years later, we did a similar thing in sharp rock ledge country where horses could not be worked. We pushed the logs over the cliffs, letting them roll until they stopped, then picked them up along the skidways. In the coldest weather, we often had to hold up cutting pine—severe cold causes trunks to freeze and become brittle, so that they snap off or split when they strike the hard ground, or a rock or tree in the way. Norway pine, though one of the strongest of conifers in this area, under ordinary circumstances, shatters easily in such conditions. However, with a little rise in temperature, and a little care in falling, you have no problem.

Ingenuity solved a lot of difficulties. One tamarack swamp lumberjack called old Jack was at first hard put to get his timber out, from his claim about a mile in the swamp. But he found a small island in the midst of the bog, where he constructed his camp. Then he built himself a wooden railroad, using straight slender poles for rails, fastened to ties. After that he made a wooden-wheeled car, sturdy enough to hold timber. With a horse for power, he was in business, and kept at it for years.

The stories of "Haywire" O'Connell would fill a book by themselves. Haywire was an everpresent but despised material that was used for all manner of emergency repairs, and Jack O'Connell came by his nickname because of his uncanny ability to make anything hold together with haywire. Big logging companies had good equipment, and if a little reinforcement was necessary, "Haywire" supplied it with emergency repairs rather than retire it to the blacksmith shop for real fixing. It wasn't a term of contempt by any means—he was liked for his cheerful spirit in trying to get the job done at whatever cost in personal sweat. He was Irish in every cell of his makeup, and looked it. Spunky, irascible, and never-say-die, when he appeared to challenge a stripling in a log-

A good-sized white pine. Notice the bark mark that was required to be chopped into every log so that it could later be identified at the sawmill. (Itasca County Historical Society)

rolling contest in the 1930's, well over fifty years old himself, the whole crowd cheered him. With one short stub of a leg, the other stiff from years of hard, grueling work in log driving and rough usage in the winter woods, Haywire dumped his fast-footed opponent. It seemed he had better control of the sudden snubbing of the log, with his short leg.

Loggers of either transient or settler variety seldom got to be Timber Barons. They were men who worked out in the timber, themselves, and spent very little time counting their money—which wouldn't have taken long in any case. They had few of the rewards and all of the worries. Fire was an ever-present specter and all-too-real danger. It wiped out whole towns—not only Hinckley, Cloquet, and White Pine, but Chisholm, Ferris, Nary, and countless small settlements and isolated cabins. No man went blithely about his work when it was reported, as in 1893, that fire raged all around Rainy lake. When there was a blaze to be fought, it was all hands in the timber. Losses were inevitable even when no homes were destroyed or lives lost—timber, buildings, supplies might go. During hot, dry seasons of high danger, there could be no logging, no railroad building, and no ties were sold. The loss of 165 stacks of hay in September, 1894 meant that fodder for fueling the hauling teams was destroyed.

Then, the weather outlook would give anybody ulcers: years when snow came late and left early, spells too warm for ice, deep snow years when men wallowed up to their armpits. Dry springs, like the one in 1897, that left logs hung in the river channels. Or the year of 1900 that had lumbermen praying for rain in April, and praying again in August that it would stop. That deluge was followed by a warm fall with no frost, and swamps were still open in late November. The problems of getting the timber cut and getting it out must have kept many a logger awake nights.

It took a breed of men that were tryers, doers, gamblers and risk takers, to stand up without whining under the "bludgeonings of chance" with heads "bloody, but unbowed." Scratch the skin of any of the old loggers, and that's what you'd find.

SNUFF JAR

4

Tamarack 'er Down

Paul's logging crew was bigger than almost everybody but Paul himself. His Seven Axemen were all six feet tall sitting down. They kept their axes sharp by holding 'em against the sides of huge boulders rolling down hill, running along beside them. It was Paul who invented the double-bitted axe—so his men could work twice as fast, cutting both ways.

One by one the old jacks "went down." From the beginning, crews varied from year to year and even from month to month, as men got tired of one cook's style and hankered for a change. Jacks are born with itchy feet, and they always seemed to want to see if the timber was bigger or the snow less deep at another camp. They didn't exactly have a rotating schedule, but year after year we'd see the same faces, and, as the season wore on, other camps in the area would see them too. Meanwhile, the restless ones from other operations would be trickling into our camp.

Stiff-neck Pete was one of the regulars who made the rounds. In any crowd, you'd know whom that name belonged to—he'd been crippled so many times I wondered what sort of haywire held him together. He had been a big, powerful brute, and still could do well enough if he wanted to, but he'd had enough vacations through workmen's compensation so that he knew all the angles. In one year, the time he spent actually working was five days.

He came to our job after his insurance claim ran out from a previous indisposition, selected a set of warm clothes from the van (which were charged against his future earnings), and settled into the bunkhouse. His first day, all went fine. On his second day, we had a spell of sharp cold. We told the men to remain in camp, since iron becomes brittle at low temperatures, and accidents happen more easily. Pete went out anyway, smeared kerosene on his hand, and froze two fingers. Back he went on rocking-chair time, and that was the last we saw of him.

He spent a lot of his recuperating periods in the bars, always ready to respond when another jack would holler "Timber!," the lumberjack lingo for "belly up to the bar." He wasn't in the best of shape at such times, and usually got shoved behind, where he would clamor for attention: "Barrrtenderrri—givit me dat 'varti peer!" (quart of beer). The hollering would continue until the bartender tossed a quart bottle over the heads of the men at the bar. Pete would tip it up and glug-glug to the last drop, let out a big satisfied belch, and say contentedly, "Tat's ta pully goot."

Black Pete Bartol, a burly, grizzled, cheerful fellow with a heavy black beard, had a problem of another sort. Though he looked like Fagin or the mad Russian monk Rasputin, he was an all-round good lumberjack. But he had one failing—a gigantic thirst that attacked him regularly, and off to town he would go on a spree. Coming back, badly hung over, he invariably met his downfall. Each time, he filled his airtight stove and lit it, and the fire blazed up and singed his whiskers. Black Pete's idea of first aid was to grab the stove and heave it out into the snow. This happened regularly.

He fared no better when we put in oil burners. Then he turned the controls up until the stove got red hot, lost his balance, and fell on top of it. Singed whiskers again, and again the flaming heater got tossed out into the snowbank.

He was with us at a shacking camp where there was a gas cookstove, and we thought all was safe at last. He'd had experience "getting the fire started" for cooking with wood, so he was quite pleased with himself when he opened the jets wide and the flames streamed up toward the ceiling. Only, another beard got burned off. With all these catastrophes, Black Pete never complained. He just laughed . . . and did it again. I don't know whether he ever learned.

The high point of his life had been during the war, when he was, he said, "Camp Push fer the Big Diamond," when so many men had been swallowed up in the armed forces that he had a chance to shine. It didn't last. With the peace, and the return of more capable men, he was demoted to piececutter. But he never tired of telling about it.

I don't know who gave Gooseneck Hans his name, but it fit. He looked like a giant whooping crane, or a scarecrow flapping in the wind. He may have been a good man in his day, but that was long before. Now he needed a job, and was working as bullcook. Along with his unusual appearance, he was blessed with a cantankerous disposition and a whiny voice, which he raised continually in complaints that the cook was unreasonable. The cook for his part was never backward about chewing the rag over the size of the tamarack kindling, a sore point with most cooks. Gooseneck Hans always lost the argument, and we'd see him flailing away with his axe at the woodpile, chopping the kindling into smaller pieces and muttering to himself.

Lumberjacks were never above dealing a little misery if they saw a chance for a good joke. Matt Strom, never a patient soul at best, was not at all pleased when the area where he and Earl Peloquin were cutting became infested with youths of the Civilian Conservation Corps, carrying gunny sacks in which they were to put pine cones. Matt hated green horns of any kind, and he thought picking pine cones was just the ridiculous kind of job they'd think of. When they spotted a wasp's nest in a nearby tree, they couldn't resist. Earl held a leaf over the entrance hole while Matt cut off the branch with the nest on it. They placed it in a gunny sack left temptingly near, tying it securely. Every now and then they nudged the sack, and got a godawful roaring. Eventually the CCC men came back and retrieved their bag, heaving it into their truck. Matt and Earl never got a report of the scene when the sack was opened, but they had a pretty fair idea of the joy it caused.

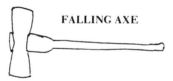

FALLING AXE

As far as Matt was concerned, nobody was exempt from his insults. When a truck driver brought word that Earl, his regular partner, would be given time off to play baseball, while Matt must continue cutting with another man, an eruption threatened. The only way peace could be restored was for the boss himself, Bliss, to agree to be Matt's partner for the time. But the harmony didn't last long. Bliss innocently got on the wrong side of the crosscut saw. Grouchy and seething already, Matt's anger burst. He quit on the spot. "Some fellas don't know which side of a saw cuts!" he shouted, and down the road he went, growling all the way.

Most of the old cutters had little education, and perhaps they wouldn't have taken any prizes even if they'd continued in school. But at their craft they were masters. Let no one make any mistake about it, cutting timber is not something learned overnight. A good timber cutter has to have a wicked eye for the woods.

There is method to felling trees, but no one formula. There can't be—there are so many variables, and so many ideas and theories, it would take a whole book to cover the subject. There are more "rules of the thumb" than most men have fingers. However, a couple of rules should never be ignored.

First, the cutter should be equipped with good, well-sharpened tools and properly fitting clothes. Second, and even more important, he must observe safety precautions: wear a hard hat! Have a basic knowledge of the kind of timber to be cut, and how it stands in relation to the lay of the land. A woodsman also needs to know something of how the timber is to be removed or skidded out of the woods.

There are problems to consider in the habits of various species, hollow trees, frost seams, windstorm split trees, size, live or dead, wet or dry condition, wind shake, frozen winter timber or pitch-and-sap-filled summer growth, heavy limb structure on one side of the tree. Height is a factor—tall trees tend to lean to the leeward from the prevailing wind. Trees grow larger in protected places, and those growing straight up are sometimes called "skybound," as their weight makes them harder to move off the stump with wedges, when felling.

(In old woods operations, as standard practice, the cutting boss had a well laid-out system, with the logging road cleared, and landings spaced at the prescribed distance for best skidding. Strips for cutters were blazed, each approximately sixty-six feet wide. This was all in preparation.)

Now the cutter comes upon the scene.

He begins by sizing up the individual tree, looking upward for loose dead branches, tangling with other tree tops, or other elements that may be a hazard. He must judge which way the tree leans, for although in general a tree will naturally fall in that direction, the cutter can steer or swing it in a quadrant up to ninety degrees from its natural line of fall. The more it leans, the less it can be steered. An experienced woodsman understands this well, but a novice should think seriously before attempting to fall a tree, steering it too far out of its natural fall line.

Of course the tree must fall into an open area. Too many woods accidents are caused by falling or raking one tree against another, causing the tree to roll, or swing sidewise, or jump backward from its stump—sometimes shooting a distance of many feet. All of these things do happen, and, in selective cutting, frequently such trees must be fallen. The experienced faller is aware of all this, and plans his work accordingly.

Another highly important factor is the wind. Its velocity and direction may vary daily, or even hourly.

After balancing these variables in his mind, the cutter approaches the tree, axe in hand. He clears away the surrounding underbrush, as well as an escape route. Next he trims the bark around the trunk where he plans to make his cut. He then takes his stance at the proper distance from the tree, and chops into its base the undercut, or "scarf."

The undercut is made in the direction of the intended fall, deep enough to assure control of its direction. It's the breaking point or fulcrum of the tree, and must be deep enough to prevent a leaning tree splitting, or "barber-chairing." This cut is placed just above the swell of the root structure.

That done, he takes up his crosscut saw, on the opposite side of the tree. (In the case of a two-man gang, the two-man crosscut is used, with one man at each end.) He begins the falling cut, two or three inches above the undercut, holding the saw in as level a plane as possible in relation to the stump. The cut is not parallel to the ground—it is perpendicular to the tree trunk.

TWO-MAN CROSSCUT SAW

Each individual's rhythmic effort is different, but the result will be the same. If the saw is properly sharpened for the species of tree, especially in the case of pine, long curls of sawdust will fly out of the rakers passing through the cut. The proper amount of pressure must be applied to the saw, and the whole body moves with the swing of the arms in rhythmic motion. This comes only with long practice.

Two men sawing together often find this a source of contention, unless they enjoy a unity of motion like dancers. Many heated battles have ensued, and friends have separated, because one man was "riding" the saw too hard, or using a jerky or sloppy motion.

Using kerosene on the saw helps reduce friction or drag. Fallers often carried a small whiskey bottle of kerosene for this purpose.

The sawing continues, on a line parellel and in close proximity to the undercut. Long, tapered wedges are driven in progressively, following the saw cut. These were usually dry, hard maple, or iron, and may now be plastic. Their purpose was to hold the cut open in case of wind swaying of the trunk, and to help topple the tree and guide its fall.

The saw approaches the undercut, but it should never pass that point. Some holding wood must be allowed, acting as a hinge, to prevent kickback or spin of the tree on its stump. If the tree is a leaner, more holding wood is left in the saw cut on the side toward which the tree is meant to fall. There may even be some cutting necessary to assure control.

The tree begins to fall.

There is ample time to take the saw out of the cut, and withdraw to the faller's safety spot. This should be a safe distance back—one tree may necessarily strike another, raking down limbs that fly backwards, or limbs may be tangled. The best place is behind another tree, out of harm's way.

It's a thrilling sight, and one I've never tired of, watching the giants of the forest strike the earth. But ironically I've also hated to see the big pines go down, every one. They were the irreplaceable jewels of the forest.

Once the tree is down, the cutter checks quickly that all loose branches caught overhead in other trees have come down. One of these, falling while the men are at work under them, spells death. That's why it is called the "widowmaker."

The next step, limbing, is almost as hazardous as felling. The axe is used for "swamping," or trimming the limbs off smoothly from the trunk. Sometimes these are caught in other branches, or bent over small trees, causing "spring poles" loaded with tension that may fly back. If an unwary swamper strikes down into the spring pole, the force of its release may throw the axe into him. Experienced men chop the spring pole from underneath, relieving the tension when possible, clearing the brush and limbs aside to provide for easy footwork.

During cold weather, in black spruce or thick-standing balsam, where the limbs were not too large, there was a faster method of limbing. By walking along the tree, swinging a three-foot-long hardwood club in long sweeps, the cutter could rapidly eliminate all limbs.

At this point, the tree trunk is ready for measuring and bucking into logs or whatever. The woodsman has his measuring pole handy—usually a slender, sturdy pole, eight feet four inches long, with carved marks at two foot intervals. (Logs are cut four inches longer than given lengths, allowing the extra for trimming lumber at the mill.) We often used this measure as a "push pole," with a sharp spike driven into its end, and a metal collar or wire wrapping to prevent splitting. This push pole was handy for tipping smaller stubborn trees against the wind, or other conditions.

Using the measure, the tree trunk is marked off into the most desirable cuts, minimizing crooks, and as long a length of straight timber as possible. Then it is sawed or bucked up. Again the wedges may be needed, to keep the saw from pinching. Often it is necessary to block up the ends of a log so it won't split in the cutting process.

Timber is sawed into logs, piling, boom timbers, mining poles, pulpwood, saw bolts, posts, or various other products. In cedar, first choice is long, straight, sound poles of specified top size. Pine bridge piling, likewise, requires not only top size, but also standard butt size. Tie trees are limbed, scored, then hewed in a long string while attached to the top of the tree, (to keep it more stable during the hewing), then cut to length.

Piling, poles, and ties were often spud-peeled and cut to size right where they fell in the woods. This required the expertise of top woodsmen, for in reality they made the finished product right there on the strip.

To get long straight poles, men sometimes had to improve on nature. This could be done by placing the bowed tree belly down, the center resting on blocks or skids with the ends up. The unsupported heavy ends were forced downwards by their own weight, straightening the timber. The opposite method could also be used, as an alternative.

It was always a good practice to fall the timber in a "cattywampus" fashion—that is, at a long diagonal to the skidding trails, putting the tree tops to either side, and keeping the trail clear. Cutting was always geared to the system of skidding and logging roads. Trees were fallen away from the main stand, or "face," of the timber. If a whole stand leaned heavily, it was often necessary to start from the back side, to let the trees fall their natural way.

Having felled the tree, and limbed and bucked it up, the cutter was by no means done. It was also his duty to stack his wood, on skids. Without this precaution, timber cut in summer for winter skidding was in danger of rotting, or freezing to the ground.

The cutter went through this process with all the trees on his strip. When it was completed, the checker, or cutting boss, came to take the count or "scale." Systems of tallying and counting that had been devised to make the job easier were especially appreciated on cold days. The simple form of four dashes with a line drawn through to represent five was widespread. Dots and dashes in a pattern were easily read. The code was: one dot to represent one, placing four dots in a square, connecting the dots with four lines, then crossing the square with an x. This made a total of ten items. This method was used mostly in counting logs, piling, poles and other items, where many individual pieces were involved on a single page in the checking book.

Deceit was rarely practiced. Most men were scrupulously honest, with pride in their work. Occasionally, though, a cutter might plug the hole in the butt of a cedar pole by rounding out the hole and fitting a plug into it. In order to make it appear uniform, he would then make a fresh cut. An experienced checker could usually detect such swindles at a glance, partly because he knew which men were likely to try them.

This is by no means the only way to fall timber. The methods are as numerous and varied as the men cutting trees. The main point is, the novice should be aware of the pitfalls. He should by all means see how it's done by the experts in his locality before wading into the forest to do battle.

The same principles of skill in woodsmanship apply when using a power chain saw—only more so. The speed at which the cuts are made can be disastrous in felling trees—a bit too deep a cut on the stump, and the tree is out of control. Kickbacks, jumping brush swipes, and many other perilous movements happen so fast the unwary operator is soon in trouble. Vigilant care in following safe practices is the only way to go.

RAKER-TOOTH GUAGE

Even the experts, in spite of their familiarity with the woods, occasionally misjudge. One busy winter we were cutting and skidding some nice White and Norway pine timber near Bass Lake. I'd spaced the cutters at fairly safe distances in relation to each other, always a wise policy in tall timber. As the logging work progressed, I often worked a spare cat, making trails for fallers in brushy areas, and clearing the roads and landings ahead. Cutters, skidders, and I usually stopped at 3 P.M. for a spot of coffee at the landing.

Highball Harry Morse, the skidding cat operator, the choker setter Norbert Perreault, and several pine cutters were at the landing already when I came up with the cat, hauling a drag of logs. One of the cutters, Big Emil Alderson, told us he was about to fall a big tree, near the landing, and for safety's sake asked us to stay away from the area for about fifteen minutes. Everyone agreed. Highball Harry took off for the woods with the skidding cat, and I told Emil I would push the logs up into piles on the landing and leave immediately, giving him time to fall his tree after we'd gone.

But something went amiss in Emil's timing.

As I pushed the logs up, above the sound of the cat's engine I could hear Big Emil pounding on his wedges. In the same moment, while backing away from the log pile I caught a glimpse of movement out of the corner of my eye. The big-limbed White Pine was coming down right toward the cat.

My first instinct was to speed up the throttle, and I hit that lever—but it was an old model with a terribly slow reverse, and was already full throttle. What happened in split seconds seemed to take hours. I was straining to get that cat (and myself under the fragile metal protector cab) back twenty feet or so out of the line of fall but there wasn't time. The huge tree was coming right at me. I knew the cab wouldn't save me.

About fifteen feet back time ran out. I kicked the hand clutch out of gear and catapulted myself out of the cat seat onto the ground, against the side of the cat farthest from the tree, hunched down on my knees with my hands covering the back of my head. In the same instant CRASH! BANG! the tree hit the cat with a shower of broken limbs practically burying me in the tangled debris.

The next thing I knew, a strange voice was speaking to me. I realized it was Big Emil, calling to ask if I was all right, while tearing the pile of broken limbs off me. The haziness cleared, and I saw his white, shocked face.

We surveyed the disaster area. The main trunk of the frozen tree, eighteen inches in diameter, had broken into several pieces across the bulldozer. I had jumped barely in time to keep myself from getting the full weight of the tree crushed right down on me. I knew then that the providence of God Almighty had saved my life, and was very thankful for it.

Actually there was very little damage. The cab of the cat was bent by the large limbs breaking over it, with the air cleaner and the hood bashed in. I felt only moderate bumps about my head, shoulders, and arms, most likely through the protection of my heavy Scotch cap and mackinaw. Blood was coming from my eyelid, but the only cause we could find was a sharp broken splinter that had flipped up after hitting the frozen ground.

Seconds later Highball Harry came up with a skid of logs, jumped off his cat and landed running as Emil and I were throwing the branches aside, shouting, "What the hell you trying to do, Emil, kill the boss?"

Poor Emil was very apologetic. A good woodsman, he had nevertheless misjudged the lean of the tree. Big pine often lean to the southeast, or the heavy limbs grow longer in that direction, toward the morning sunlight. For some reason, this tree leaned north, toward a small natural opening which we had cleared into a landing. He had tried to force the tree the wrong way with his wedges, but a slight gust of wind had pushed it backwards—right onto the cat (and me) at the landing.

Emil lived only one more year. He had a heart attack driving his car from town on a cold night, and was frozen stiff when we found him.

Part of the expertise of certain top woodsmen was due to their skill at saw filing.

Saw filing was an art of its own, whether done by the camp saw filer or the sawyer himself. The camp saw filer had the advantage of a warm, comfortable shop, with all the necessary equipment. Even so, many a timber cutter could do as well or better under the various conditions he had to contend with.

Basically, the shop tools were a board clamp or vise which held the saw; a hammer, swedge (or spring set gauge), raker tooth gauge, and good sharp files.

The cutter doing "stump filing" laid his saw on a flat stump. Then, with hammer and swedge, he tapped the cutting teeth to the desired set. His next step was to saw a vertical cut into each of two small stumps at a convenient height for filing—waist high, or thereabouts. He placed the saw in these cuts, teeth up, to hold it while he pulled the raker gauge with a file clamped into it across the top of the cutting teeth, making sure they were all even length. Next he used the raker gauge, and filed the rakers down to the desired depth, slightly shorter than the cutting teeth. When this was done, he filed them to a sharp point. It doesn't sound simple, and it wasn't.

Good filers often put a little hook into the raker teeth, to aid in the removal of sawdust from the cut.

Finally, the cutting teeth were sharpened with a file, held at proper angle, to a needle point—but no more.

There were men who used a fine stone, and honed the filed edges of the teeth lightly, as a finishing touch. The better the saw was filed, the faster and easier it cut.

I once had a lesson in this. We had a portable shacking camp, consisting of some ten or twelve neatly-built four-man capacity camps. These were on skids so that we could move them from place to place in the woods, for cutters. The men liked to "batch"—that is, live and cook alone, or perhaps with one other man as a partner. The sun was setting when my brother Bill and I stopped in camp to see if the men needed groceries.

When we entered the cabin of sixty-eight-year-old Oscar Lahti, he was filing his saw—in the dark corner, facing the wall, without glasses.

I wondered about it, and from the peculiar look on Bill's face, judged that he was amused, too.

No, Oscar said, in response to Bill's question, he had enough groceries. Before we could say more, another cutter, Lars Nelson, came to the open door and looked in at Oscar, who was still busily filing with his back to us.

Lars said what we were thinking: "How can you see to file your saw in a dark corner without glasses?"

Old Oscar turned sidewise, spat into his coffee-can spittoon, and answered gruffly, "Who da heck needs glassis to file da saw?" He kept right on filing.

Bill and I discussed this on the way home, and decided that Oscar could file in the dark. Because of his many years of experience, he knew precisely how much pressure to exert against the teeth, at what angle to hold the file, and how many strokes to use to bring the tooth to needlepoint sharpness.

Next day I made it a point to keep an eye on Oscar's sawing. He tackled a great White Pine near the logging road—near the same landing where, a few days later, the tree fell on the cat. I could see that he had sharpened the saw to perfection. The sawdust was flying out in two-inch long thick curls as he swished away on his saw. His tall, lanky, strung-together body moved with a grace that belied his loose-hung appearance, and his bright blue eyes held a very intense expression. He could really swing that saw.

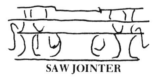

SAW JOINTER

That particular tree he was cutting was a beauty. It produced six sixteen-foot logs and a twelve-foot, making a total of 108 lineal feet from one tree. I believe he could easily have taken another ten-foot small log from the top. I often wish I would have learned Oscar's secret of filing his saw.

Oscar was one of the finest of his kind, and a pleasant fellow around camp. But, like most jacks, he was his own worst enemy. All winter he'd made good money, and saved it. When spring came, he felt the powerful urge to go to Duluth, the usual springing-out place for many of the old jacks. But he wanted to go in style, and the desire of his heart was to have a white buckskin jacket like the one my brother Donald wore. Oscar tried it on in the bunkhouse "just to see," and then he absolutely refused to take it off. He insisted he couldn't bear to give it up, Donald must let him have it. Donald gave in, and even drove him to town on the first leg of his journey. They celebrated his freedom with a few drinks and a sauna at my father's house.

In a glow at the evening's end, Oscar decided Bigfork was a pleasant place to be; he'd spend a few days there, and go to Duluth with Don at the week's end.

Three days later, when Don finally tracked him down in Bigfork, he was almost unrecognizable. He was hunched in a corner of the bar, his buckskin jacket black from sleeping in the coal room of the Village Hall (which was the jacks' unofficial flophouse), broke, and sick. It was the old lumberjack story repeated once more.

Another high-powered cutter was Carl Bergeson. He carried about a dozen one-man crosscut saws neatly stored in the trunk of his Pontiac. There was a saw filed and set for every variable condition that could occur by any stretch of the imagination—some for White and Norway pine, for cold and warm weather, and the same for spruce, balsam, cedar, popple, or birch. He cut 'em all.

Though he was a small but muscular man, he could compete with the top cutters anywhere in the area. Added to his menagerie of saws was a simple tool he called his "Swede helper," (Carl was Norwegian), for cutting these big pine trees down. This device was a pointed steel rod with a loop at the top, which he drove into the frozen ground on the opposite side of the tree from his own position. To the loop he attached a sturdy rubber band (probably a slice from a big heavy-duty inner tube), fastened to the end of his saw.

Getting himself into the proper position and tension, the rubber band pulled against him, returning the saw with an even smooth stroke. It kept the saw from whipping or slapping against the sides of the cut, as if there were another man trained to do exactly what the head sawyer wanted. Then you ought to have seen him go at it. With this mute assistant on the end of his saw, Carl could produce about half again as much as the top-flight cutters. And there was no argument about who was riding the saw too hard.

In due time, however, another serious change in timber cutting took place. The advent of the power chain saw made more difference in lumberjacking than anything else in its whole long history. This "thing" (as they at first hostilely referred to it) brought an end to the old woodsman's creed of living out in the timber as if he were a part of it.

It burst on the industry overnight. How long ago the concept came into being I have no idea, but I saw one in a museum at Lincoln, New

Mexico that was surely the earliest prototype of a handpowered chain saw to be found anywhere.

The old jacks didn't take it lightly. In fact, they objected whole-heartedly. Perhaps it was not so much that they foresaw their own demise from the woods, as that they didn't like all that racket in the timber. They complained that you couldn't put a tree down where you wanted to as skillfully as with the old crosscut. Besides, they were too dangerous to monkey with. A man could get killed, with one of those darn things buzzing the trees off so fast you couldn't tell which way to run for safety when the tree did fall. Anyway, who but a pack of wizards could ever keep the darn pesky things running?

For these and innumerable other reasons, the old jacks shook their heads and said, "It'll never work."

They were right on most counts, except the last. A daring new breed of men made them work.

It is my humble belief that a greater volume of timber was fallen by men in the prime pine-cutting era with two-man crosscuts than has fallen in an equal time with chain saws. However, this may be an unfair statement—the old timers had much better timber to work with. But it's a fact that John Erickson once beat a chain saw in a contest.

The chain saws changed the jacks.

No doubt there are parallel situations, but this is how it happened in our camp.

We had about twelve good men falling pine in our crew, in the late winter of 1951. The snow was waist deep, and the men were growing tired. We tried to ease the situation by adding extra crews, and bull-dozing trails for the men so they could get to the trees.

Along with the jacks, my brothers Art and Bill kicked up quite a fuss over my monkeying with these chain saws. I used two McCullochs around the woods for my own work on landings around the mill, blow-downs, and so on, and even felled some of the sacred pines occasionally. Art and Bill raised the complaint that the old jacks were perturbed. They said, "You'll get killed fooling around with those things, and besides, the men may walk out of the woods if you keep at it."

Granted, our first experience with the contraptions had been a failure. We'd experimented with one of the earliest models, an unwieldy monster that needed two men to handle it. The powerful man, Vern Lorenz, and his partner, agile Fuzzy Vail, who had tried it brought it back to the camp and slung it on the blacksmith's pile of junk iron. "If you want to cut timber with that thing, go ahead," they said. "But not us." But the newer saws were much improved.

My contention was that the time of change had come, whether we liked it or not. Now we must move ahead as our father would have done. The old generation of jacks were fading away, their places being taken by mechanical monsters.

The matter was hung there.

But the efforts made in the heavy snow could not compensate for loss in production. We simply couldn't get the timber out. One morning I told Bill, "I'm going to go cut some trees down for each cutter or two-man gang. It will alleviate the situation somewhat, and at least relieve the old fellows of the backbreaking job of getting the big pine down." Bill conceded that it would be a great help to the tired men.

I started by cutting down some big trees in the worst brushy cutting area, for the least contentious of the men, Jonas Tasanen. He was elated that the trees went precisely where they were supposed to go. When I'd fallen enough to keep him busy bucking them up for a couple of days, old Pete Westlie came hurrying up, and stood there amazed. His eyes bugged out as he watched the last trees fall.

Poor old Pete was one of nature's noblemen, but his heart was failing, and he had to pop a dynamite pill every so often—I'd often seen him do this while catching his breath, leaning against a tree until his condition stabilized. At any rate, Pete, a very logical, good natured fellow, said with Jonas, "I couldn't-a believed it." Pete asked if I'd come over to his strip and cut some extra-big White Pine, three to four feet on the stump. I sure would.

WEDGES

HOLDER WITH
WHISKEY BOTTLE
OF KEROSENE

I did cut down the big trees for Pete, and knock off the butt logs to make it easier sawing for him, then lopped off the big limbs. He was all smiles, knowing that he would double his earnings from the extra boost. Before I'd finished with Pete, here came Carl Bergeson, a true son of Norway, to see what was going on. I believe he was most dead-set against anything beating his system. However, I noticed the twinkle in his eyes as he invited me over to his strip to cut some more big trees. He was younger than the others, and fairly feisty as we came up to his timber.

I realized he'd prepared to test me out, when he pointed to a stake where he wanted to fall a heavy leaner. This could only be done if he'd use his wedges, helping me tip the tree where he had designated. He agreed to drive the wedges, and down it went—right on his stake! Carl was so tickled that he pumped my hand again and again.

Next day Pete bought one of my saws, and I loaned Jonas the other. Big Emil Alderson, not to be outdone, ordered me to get him a saw. The next fall, Carl Bergeson came to camp with three chain saws in the back of his Pontiac. Never did I see his "Swede helper" again.

May Carl, Pete, and Jonas strike me down with a thunderbolt from Valhalla, where they now sit yarning, if this isn't exactly how it happened.

The old men did an about-face, and took to the chain saws like ducks to water. Within a few years the woods were just buzzing with the wild racket, and clouds of oily smoke hung about on a frosty morning—a far cry from what the men had predicted. The old jacks proved that they could accept the change. A new kind of competition sprang up: whether the McCulloch, Pioneer, Titan, Homelite, Clinton, Mall, Disston, or whatever model or individual choice each preferred, was best. No longer was there much question about Simons, Atkins, or Sandvik saw blades. More debate appeared in discussions of how to file their Oregon chains.

The old jacks stood by for quite a long time. They made a lot more money, but perhaps this was their downfall. Many of them hit the bottle a little too hard, on their new-found prosperity. Consequently I began to hear: "This oily smoke is getting me down;" "too much vibration on the saw;" "Think I'll go down." One by one, they left the camps until we had no more need of running a camp.

The new crew was all on wheels—speeding through the woods with all kinds of rigs: foreign jalopies, cars, and pickups. It was a big change from earlier years, when men who drove to the woods were called "car tramps," and were unwelcome. Those who then had cars had kept them a safe walking distance from camp, so as not to molest the horses, and certainly not lure any men away from camp life. Those who transgressed soon got their walking papers.

One of the last to leave was Carl Bergeson. He loved the woods life like a true woodsman. But when my brother Bill was felled by a White Pine, Carl, by then in his seventies, retired from the woods. The next year he passed on to join the ranks of the lumberjacks in the pine hills of Valhalla.

Now it is finally so mechanized, with rubber-tired skidders and front-end loaders chasing one another all over the woods, replacing the horses, cats, and jammers, it's a totally different ball game. Loggers now rely on the tree shear that snips the tree off its roots with a big scissors, and stacks the carcasses in windrows, where a monstrous grapple skidder grabs up a bundle of full-length trees that even the legendary Paul Bunyan would marvel at. This machine drags the trees, limbs and all, to a yarding area (no longer a landing or skidway or rollway). There, an even more monstrous monolith chews or spins off the bark and limbs, and sends the denuded tree on to another section that grinds it into chips, blowing them into huge tank van trailers. These are in turn hauled to the various hungry mills, by a constant stream of many-wheeled trucks, the drivers communicating as radio buddies about all the details or dangers to look out for, on the road.

The mills devouring the huge piles of chips like hungry behemoths through programmed departmental structures, complexes of various chemical digestive processes and all these modern wonders are computerized. In the end, a bewildering array of products are spewed out: building board materials, paper products, plastics, and all sorts of prestigious inventions which we got along without for ages, but now (the advertisers tell us) we desperately need. The future promises greater hopes for even better things.

No more is heard the ring of the woodsman's axe, or the singing, soughing buzz of his saw in the pines. This is a sad day, for me. I never wanted to see the last of the lumberjacks "go down."

Keewatin Co. Farm Camp seven miles south of Bigfork. The farm gardens produced potatoes, onions, 'bagas, cabbage, etc., to feed the men in the company camps in winter. (Itasca County Historical Society)

5

Timber on the Move

When Paul was just a year old, his daddy gave him a little blue ox for a pet. Paul named him "Babe." Babe grew just as fast as Paul, and he got to be BIG: seven axehandles and a plug of tobacco between the eyes. He was a real help to Paul, skidding. When the trails and roads and rivers got too crooked, Paul would pick up one end, and Babe would pick up the other, and they'd pull on them to straighten out the kinks.

Teamsters were the elite of the camp. They got paid more than the regular crew, and they deserved it. They had to get up an hour before the rest of the men—four a.m.—to care for their animals and get them ready for the day's work. The day's end found them straggling back to camp much later than anybody else. This understandably affected their dispositions. Tired teamsters fell into their bunks wanting nothing but sleep, and were something less than amused when other men wanted to talk or play cards. Because of this, in earliest camps, they sometimes slept with their beasts. In several camps of our area, they had a separate bunkhouse known as "the growl house."

In the beginning, oxen were used as draft animals in the woods. They had certain advantages over horses: greater power and the ability to subsist on hay, without much grain. This was a big consideration, as feed for large numbers of animals would constitute a formidable problem in logistics. Oxen required less care, and, pound for pound, pulled bigger loads. Cost was a factor: an ox team might cost $100, and the yoke could be chopped from a piece of log. In contrast, for a good team of horses a man might pay $200 to $500, with $100 added for a set of harness. Coupled with this was the stolid endurance of oxen. They could be worked in wetter places, often wallowing up to their bellies in the mud. Finally, if an ox got hurt, or broke a leg, it wasn't a total loss; he could be eaten.

Len and Dutch Knotts grew up herding oxen around with a gore stick, or goad, doing farm and logging work. A certain amount of training went into this. To start, they placed the yoke on the animals' necks, and tied their tails together in order to keep the beasts from turning around and displacing the yoke. The next step was to hook a small log or sled to the pull chain, and coax the team along with a bucket containing a mouthful of cracked corn or oats. It didn't take long for the beasts to get the idea, and with a little prodding for "gee" (right turn) and "haw" (left turn) from the gore stick—a short straight stick with a nail in the end—they could graduate to more efficient efforts.

There was no doubt that working with oxen took a certain amount of practice, as well as grinding persistence and energy. Cal DeLaittre reported how Wes Day screened applicants for that job. When one would-be teamster presented himself, Wes asked, "Oh, B'God. How do I know you can handle oxen? Here, you show me. I'll be the ox, and you show me how you'd drive." Wes handed the man a goad stick, and bent over on his hands and knees.

The man gingerly waved the goad in the direction of the boss' rear, and said timidly, "Get up!"

Wes shook his head. "Oh, B'God, you'll never do."

But the man's need was urgent, so a few days later he applied again. Wes again pretended to be the ox. This time the man said firmly, "Get up, damn you!" and rammed Wes with the goad in the appropriate part of his anatomy. Wes jumped up. "Oh, B'God, you'll do!"

A single ox worked best when skidding small logs, but with a "go-devil" sled two were better. On large loads, four were needed to pull the sleigh. Three teams of oxen were the most effective number—two working and one resting.

Oxen are not bright, sensitive animals, and working with them was often frustrating. Teamsters were a colorful breed, many of them recluses who kept apart from their fellow men and operated on a short fuse. The language the ox teamster used in handling his beasts was sizzling enough to curdle the pancake batter at forty paces, and was mostly original with each man.

One such man, Johnny Enright, was heir to a milling company, but seemed to have no contact with his family. His oxen were his life, and a miserable life it was. Sometimes, long hours after the rest of the crew was happily in their bunks and snoozing, Johnny could be heard out in the woods, where his team was hung up on a stump by the draw pin, hollering half the night in words to curl the listener's hair. It would be hours before he could get the load free, for the stubborn beasts never moved fast. Back in the bunkhouse men covered their ears with their pillows to shut out the noise until he would finally come in at two o'clock in the morning. Since he had to start the day again in a matter of only a couple of hours, it was well to give him a wide berth.

Untrained oxen were even worse to deal with. When "Uncle Tom" Neveux sold a pair, for $110, to be delivered in Grand Rapids, he recruited his son Joe and young Fred Peloquin to make the trip from Bigfork. The old tote road went by way of the Farm Camp, then seemingly from lake to lake—past Club House Lake, on to Spider and Trout Lake, and thence to Grand Rapids.

It started well enough—the animals were sojourning in a barn to protect them from flies, and permitted themselves to be yoked. But there was no means of driving them, only herding or chasing them, and that was the source of the trouble.

Of course a packsack full of grub was needed for the journey, and the youths saw no reason to carry it when the oxen could do it more easily. However, the oxen didn't agree, and they wanted none of the excursion, anyway. They showed their displeasure by walking fast until they found an opening in the timber that overhung the road; then they would turn off at gallop, plunge into the timber, and bolt back through the woods toward their old home.

There was no way the lads could overtake them until the foolish animals would try to pass the same tree on opposite sides, and get stuck. Then the panting escort could catch up to them, but they refused to back up until the boys pounded their noses enough to get the idea across. Pointed once more toward their destination, they watched their chance, and performed the same maneuver at the next gap.

The end of the first day found the weary entourage at Trout Lake, footsore and disgruntled. The only shelter offered was an abandoned camp, with a signboard stating that eighty-two men had died there from smallpox (Fred thought the year was 1889, but wasn't positive). With no rope to secure the oxen, they chopped trees into the road, forming a rude corral.

If they had hoped for a good night's rest, they were disappointed. Mosquitoes in unmerciful swarms attacked them at daybreak next morning. Wearily they continued their trek, and found deliverance when they were twelve miles from the teeming metropolis: they reached a homesteader Joe knew.

This man, one Frank Freestone, had pity on them. He fed them, and hitched up his horses for a trip to the big city himself. So, while one youth chased the oxen ahead of the team, the other rode in luxury in the wagon. The day was Sunday, but the saloons, stores and other business places of the town were wide open. Their charges delivered, Joe and Fred returned to Bigfork.

The incredible part of this saga is that they undertook this safari just for the fun of it.

The greater intelligence, speed, and versatility of horses made it inevitable that they would displace the slow, stubborn oxen. Both served well in their respective positions in the history of logging, and there were times when the drivers came to fisticuffs trying to settle the hash of which were most valuable. Bullwhackers and horsemen have never been able to decide the issue.

The feeding of horses was an important detail. High quality hay was essential to the good health and workability of the animals. Dusty of moldy hay, which caused respiratory problems, or "heaves," was to be avoided. For energy, three times a day the animal was given oats, with some corn, the amount regulated by the size of the horse and the work he was doing. Occasionally, when the horses needed a laxative, bran was fed.

Caution was exercised in watering the horses—it was not to be done when they were "hot" from work.

Horses hauling heavy loads had to be given a rest often, to get their wind. In cold weather, horses were susceptible to colds or frosted lungs, and had to be driven with discretion. It was dangerous to let them work too hard, or strain too greatly: they could get "wind broken." When they perspired, they were stopped for rest periods and covered with blankets so they would not chill. Falling wet snow often meant horses were blanketed and taken to the barn, to prevent illness. No one minimized the importance of the horses, and a good barn boss supervised and insisted on the best of care for them. It was often said that better care was taken of horses than of the men in the camps.

There was some debate as to what made a good teamster, some insisting that Irish or Norwegians were the best. Actually, there were good teamsters in all nationalities. Usually what was required was a cool-tempered and quiet-natured man, with good understanding of animals—mostly just good ole horse sense. Bullock drivers had to have patience and determination. Bullwhackers had to let off a little steam every so often to get the bulls to move; their cussing was an art.

Horses to supply the needs were bought from anywhere. Devils Lake, North Dakota was a prime market, and at times they were brought from southern Minnesota or Wisconsin. They had to be big, strong, tough, and lively, with plenty of endurance. The one-ton Percherons were good sleigh-haulers and road horses, and were found at most camps—mostly black, with some roans and bays and grays. Although Belgians became more popular later, and a few Clydesdales were brought in, the dependable Percherons remained the favorites.

At times wild broncs from the west were bought, and broken to harness. Tough and wild though they were, they could be good work horses under careful handling. But prairie horses brought to the woods were likely to be nervous. They were quick to take fright, spooked easily, and were wild as deer. The calm, gentler native horse was far easier to work.

Seemingly teamsters saved their best nature for their animals. Often they lovingly braided the manes and tails, and tied bright ribbons in them, as though they were their best girl friends. But they were frequently notoriously quarrelsome toward their fellow man. The Heffner brothers, Andrew and Fritz, were a case in point. They always worked together, and fought with each other bitterly the whole time, for no discernible reason except cantankerous deviltry. No one was present when matters came to a head. Andrew walked to town and told the sheriff: "Well, I killed Fritz. But you'll never find him." Privately the sheriff thought that it was no great loss, and it might have been all to the good if both had been killed, but a search was instituted. Fritz was never found, but they took Andrew's word for the situation, and sent him off to sit in the booby hatch for the rest of his life.

Although Paul Fournier loved and cared for horses with skill, he had less affection for humans. He spent seven years in the penitentiary for murder: as a hired assassin, he killed a father and daughter for $500. With Paul in the pokey in Stillwater, another teamster reasoned that he would have no need for his stove, and helped himself to it. But Paul was released unexpectedly. He came storming to his neighbor, demanding the return of his property. Not wishing to give it up, the neighbor shot him. Exit one more teamster.

No one argued with Michael O'Dowd either. A surly fellow, he was a fearsome sight, being two or three inches taller than six feet, and a yard or more wide. What was even more impressive, he carried a .44. With this armament, he always refused to turn out on a trail or grade. Whomever he met would find himself looking into the large bore of his gun and being told, "Halt. You walk around." This the other traveler meekly did. As far as is known, nobody ever disputed his right of way, even when the snow was neck deep.

A man of a different stripe, who has probably handled more horses than any other living teamster, is Leonard Dickinson. He started early—

when he was twelve years old, he sold an ox that he owned for $35, borrowed $15 from his grandmother, and bought a horse. That started his long love affair with these intelligent companions who put their hearts into serving men. Dickinson is raising some fine horses to this day, at his Buena Vista ranch.

It took enormous effort on the part of horses and men to get the timber out of the woods. In the eastern states, logging sleds were developed to haul the big loads. The front sled was rigged with a pole, or tongue, and a crossbeam or bolster laid across the runners, with a roller holding the front end of the runners in place by tonkin pins. The rear sled was made in a similar manner, attached to the front sledge beam with a stub pole. Later, cross chains were used to trail the rear sled.

"Bunks" or "rockers" which supported the logs were big, squared timbers resting on the beams, held in place with large iron pins known as king pins. They were placed in holes drilled through both the center of the beam and the rocker. The rocker bottom was shaped so that its under side sloped upward from the center toward the ends. An iron plate between, greased for easier turning of the loaded sled on curves, rested on the beam.

These sleds were continually improved to permit bigger loads as logging advanced to Michigan, Wisconsin, and finally Minnesota. Foundries made many special castings, such as the "Hinckley knees" that were fastended to the runners that supported the beams of the sleds. Special truss straps were added to hold the beam rigidly in place, and plates to protect the ends of the runners. Heavy iron shoes helped to make the runners slide, and prevent wear of the bottom wood.

There were special chains to hold the logs on the rockers, with a round hook and a fid hook. These were called "corner binds." They

ROUND HOOK   **FID HOOK**

ran through holes bored in the rockers, and held the outside bottom logs securely in place. When hauling eight-foot logs, ties, or pulpwood, the rockers were removed and a long timber rack was installed on the sleigh. The timber was then loaded crosswise.

In Minnesota the "sleds" somehow became "sleighs," and kept that name until they vanished into oblivion at the end of the sleigh-haul era. They were made in varied sizes and designs, according to the needs of different logging companies. Some were light sleighs, with five-foot gauge or spread of runners; some, for heavy-duty hauling, were 7'4". When steam haulers came into use, sleighs with eight-foot gauge runners were built.

The wood parts were usually from well-seasoned choice white or burr oak, but rockers came from timbers right in the logging woods. They had to be heavy enough to support big loads, and ran from eight feet on small stuff to sixteen feet wide on the biggest sleighs.

Factory-built sleighs could be purchased. However, the camp wood butcher could replace most of the wooden parts, and the blacksmith could contrive the iron. The blacksmith also made many other pieces of special equipment—bridles, toggles, trip links, bitch links, along with whipple trees (a few said "whiffle trees"), eveners, canthooks, peaveys, tongs, log hooks, pickaroons, and a host of other gadgets, right in his shop.

The sleighs were big to withstand heavy loads. In order to handle them, many horses were needed. Four-horse teams were commonly used, and, in rougher terrain, with upgrades, six-horse hitches weren't unusual.

To make the sleighs run easier, a new road surface was developed: ice.

The ice road needed certain equipment. The first item was the rutter, or rut cutter, of two long timbers set eight feet apart (or the width of the sleighs), with curved knives fastened on the bottom that sliced parallel ruts in the road surface. Ten or twelve horses pulled the rut cutter, making a level cut through sod, brush and roots. When the snow came, the rutter was used only to clear the ruts, and the water tank began its operations.

The water tank was a huge wooden tank on sleighs, with a hole stopped by a wooden plug at each of its four corners. Hauled over the road, the spray of water into the ruts mingled with the snow, and froze, creating a slippery, glassy surface. On successive trips, the ice was built up sufficiently to allow the sleighs to haul logs, eventually becoming a foot thick. This heavy layer melted slowly when the break-up came, with the result that hauling could continue far into spring. This may have been the origin of the saying that Northern Minnesota, with its inclement weather, has "nine months of winter and three months of poor sledding." Hardly any hauling was done before December, and by January there would be a foot of ice, with hauling going full tilt.

Frank Werthner worked on the water tank, and a miserable detail it was. For obvious reasons, it was night work. And it was cold. The chore of filling the tank was managed by a barrel hung on a rope to which one team was hitched, on the far side. The barrel slid down a slide into a water hole chopped in the lake ice. (In places where no lake or stream was handy, they sometimes blasted out a big waterhole in a swamp, and cribbed it up, so that water could be drawn from it to fill the icing tank.) The barrel had to be poked into the water, with a pole. When it sank, it was drawn up full, and the horse pulled it up the slide again to the open space on the top of the tank. It emptied into the tank, and the whole process was repeated until the tank was full. None of this was much fun for the crew, especially when their fellow jacks were enjoying the cozy warmth of the bunkhouse.

Filled, the contraption was hauled down the road, with the plugs out and the water drizzling into the ruts. No need to turn around—the special sleigh had two tongues, and the teams were simply unhitched and hooked on the other end of the tank to reverse direction. Some fancier tanks had wood-burning heaters, to keep the ice from clogging the tank.

A loaded tank weighed about as much as a dinosaur, and when Frank and his teamster, Tom Brady, had it half loaded one night, it began to sink in the lake. Frank yanked out the plugs, but the sled went through the ice, though the tank floated.

By hitching the lead team on a block and line in front of the pole team, they managed to get it out. But they were out of business, until, by cutting several long spruce and freezing them into the ice, they eventually managed to get back on the ice.

Wise bosses saw to it that a sleigh haul was never more than six miles. At that distance, with two turns, the team would cover twenty-four miles in a day, and that was plenty. If possible, loggers tried to hold the daily trip down to sixteen miles. An eight-mile haul was too long for two trips. Tired horses were that much more likely to get "sluiced." On a shorter haul, with more teams coming and going, teamsters had to watch for "turnout" places to pass, when loaded sleighs met empties.

Besides being hilly, roads sometimes crossed lakes. This was always hard going for the horses, as there was no "give" in such a haul. No easy places, and always pulling on a level, is hard on horses. Lakes had another disadvantage: to combat drifting, it was necessary to plow oftener.

Wet swamps could be crossed by "corduroy;" timbers laid crosswise close together, frozen in to make a mat.

On an iced road, a four-horse team could move a surprisingly large, heavy load. The problem was in getting it started. Usually the sleigh was spotted for loading with the tongue or pole canted off to the side.

When the load was ready for the haul, the teamster would "talk" to the horses, swinging the leaders to haul on the canted pole while the pole team dug in for a hard pull. This was called "racking the sleigh." The runners swung sidewise and got into motion. From the moment teams began to tighten the tugs (or traces), workmen were striking the runners with heavy wooden mallets. The jarring aided the teams to get the sleigh moving. On a cold morning, an extra boost was often given by hitching a swing team to a "luff," or snatch block. Here a block and tackle were fastened to the hind knee of the sleigh, the dead end of the line fastened to a tree or stump. With a sharp whistle or signal the teams all got down for the haul. When the load started, the luff teamster had to be quick about unhitching.

The great pressure of racking and starting the loads meant that the pole and front roll attached to the runners had to be rigged of sturdy material. But once the load was started, it slid along the iced ruts with no trouble, as a rule. The steel runners screeched and "scrowled" against the cold snow or ice, signalling a long way down the road that a load was coming. The teamsters called out commands to the horses: "Hiup" or "Giddyup" to speed up a lagging animal or team in a tough spot; but more often than not they spoke in softer tones and made a chirping sound similar to a chipmunk, as they fingered the lines while balancing their feet on the front roll. Mingled with these sounds, the creaking of the harness, the jingling of the trace chains, and the blowing and occasional snorting of the horses made crude music for the teamsters.

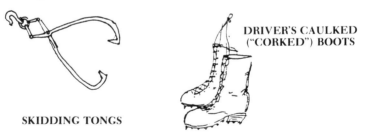

DRIVER'S CAULKED ("CORKED") BOOTS

SKIDDING TONGS

The trust and understanding between a man and his team were something to marvel at. Fred Peloquin saw an awesome example of it when, as top loader, it was his custom to ride to town with the last load of the week, to spend Sunday at his home. The road passed over a long, gradual hill. About halfway up this hill, the teamster, known only as "George," allowed his team to stop and rest. Fred wondered a bit: though the team was plainly winded, it seemed a poor place, since they would have an uphill pull to get started again, if indeed they could get the load moving.

After a few minutes rest, George began talking to the team, and Fred could see the pole team stepping around as though looking for the best foothold. George gave them a command, and they strained into their collars and pulled with all their might. At the same time, George spoke to the leaders, who literally sprang into their collars with a very audible slap. The four horses gave it everything they had, and the load began to move—slowly at first, but soon slipping along at regular speed. It was just another example of the unstinting response these noble animals give.

It seemed that most sleigh roads, when they got to the foot of a hill, turned. Not a wide, sweeping turn (logging roads were not that fancy). Sometimes sleighs would jump the ruts on the turn.

It is easy to imagine a loaded sleigh careening down an iced log-ging-road hill, as an unstoppable object. Safety braking devices were needed. The simplest, used by small loggers, was the "rough lock," a chain wrapped and tied around the sleigh runners, to slow it down on the grades. Larger companies made a practice of sanding the hills, or having the "road monkey" put down little bundles of hay in the ruts. For this purpose the hay was in small packages, to prevent the runners pushing it out. Road monkeys also had the job of cleaning manure out of the ruts.

Without these precautions, the possibility of serious accident was great—the teamster had to be a bit of a daredevil.

Accidents in the woods were rare, but this was due to the alertness of the teamster and the road monkey—especially the teamster. If the grade seemed to need attention, it wasn't unusual to hear the teamster holler ahead for the road monkey to get some hay down, or fill in some snow. No one could afford to get careless. Not only might the load spill, but the lives of both men and horses could be forfeited.

Every teamster had a tale to tell of a hair-raising narrow escape. On one occasion, when the rough lock broke loose on the grade and the load took off, the driver, Leonard Dickinson, was thrown onto the pole, in the middle of the horses. The momentum of the load flung it on the front stake, and the load of cedar ties pitched forward onto the horses. Miraculously, this was a quiet, steady team. They did not panic, even when the timber struck them. What could have been a fatal disaster ended with no one badly hurt.

The use of sand for braking power was surprisingly effective, some-times too much so. A road monkey having been ordered to improve matters on a hill arrived with a pail of hot sand just as Spike Patrow's load, coming down the grade, went out of control. The road monkey dashed the sand into the ruts, thickly, and stopped the load dead. But Spike didn't stop. He made a high dive from the mountain of timber and landed on the eveners. The lead team tightened up with a jerk, and again Spike was airborne. Being a lumberjack, he lived through it, and nothing was lost, except possibly Spike's temper. I would assume that that road monkey left for healthier parts without delay.

Nearly every year, a sign of spring was the ice giving way under a team. Usually the horses were saved, but not always. One logging story concerns a teamster who was drowned himself, when he dived into the water to unhitch his horses. He had nearly released them, but couldn't quite complete it. One careless teamster lost a team through lake ice by taking them over a reef which a more experienced man would have detected. It was a tragedy that could have been avoided.

Minnesota's unpredictable weather could cause havoc in other ways. One year, when the spring thaw came early, Charles Bibeau and others at the camp had to shovel snow into the sleigh ruts, so that the teams could haul at night on the crust. There was frenzied activity at nearly every camp as spring approached: the bosses feeling the pressure of the deadline, and the men beginning to feel "stakey" and getting juiced up for their annual spring "blow-out."

Northern Minnesota certainly had the right condition for the ice road sleigh haul. Long winters, cold weather, and much flat terrain were all conducive to the development of the system. No doubt it was a factor in the rapid logging of Minnesota's virgin timber. There was a certain competition over "picture loads." One outfit at Blackduck even hauled tandem sleigh loads with six-horse teams on a good iced road, up to a record of 56,000 board feet. On an average, the load for four horses ran about 7,000 to 10,000 board feet, which weighed twenty-five to thirty tons. A load of 5,000 board feet on big sleighs with eight-foot runner spread and sixteen-foot rockers, was immense. At ten thousand pounds per thousand feet, it would weigh 50,000 pounds, the equivalent of half a boxcar load. Normally, a pulp load was twelve cords (six double cords) of eight-foot sticks.

The name of Jack McDonald will go down in teamster history. He was preternaturally strong, and one evening when one of his horses dropped while he was still some distance from the camp, he performed the feat that brought his fame. Unhooking the incapacitated horse from the traces, Jack took his place, shouldering the neck yoke and pulling with the remaining horses. From that time on, he was known as Jack-the-Horse.

He even carried the title out of the logging woods and into his later career as a bartender in Deer River. His boss was a man who looked much like him, and this led to trouble. A lumberjack customer, following the custom of leaving his paycheck with the saloon keeper, returned later, somewhat befuddled, for a bit of cash on account. Jack, who was on duty, had never seen the man, and refused his request. The customer was enraged. He thought that the man who refused was the same man as the one to whom he'd given his stake, and that an attempt was being made to cheat him. He got a gun, returned to the saloon, and shot Jack-the-Horse to death.

But Jack's memory will never be forgotten. His name was given to the lake where it all took place, Jack-the-Horse Lake, eight miles from Bigfork.

Jonathan Moors was a man who loved horses. According to his son A D he "wanted them around all the time, whether or not there was anything for them to do. Even putting roofing on a building, he was not happy unless he had a horse looking at him." Despite the miserable conditions of the winter sleigh-hauls, he was happy, as long as he had four beauties doing his bidding. The teamster's job was a cold one. In the below-zero weather, with no protection from the wind as you held your arms steady, fingering the lines in canvas-gloved hands while standing on the roll of the sleigh—you had to like what you were doing.

A D naturally became a teamster as well, on a sleigh haul to the river, where a steep grade was always kept sanded and hayed. He broke over the hill in a snowstorm, expecting the road to be ready—but someone had blundered. The ruts were slick as glass.

There was no way he could hold the load. It pushed the horses, and they ran wildly ahead of it. A D figured that he was doing at least thirty miles an hour with four horses ahead of him, and a turn at the bottom. As he swung around the curve half of his load spilled. "Sluiced!" When he got stopped, he was in no happy mood, though after he got over the scare he said philosophically that his logs had been unloaded free.

A D could survive a near-disaster and laugh about it, but seeing animals abused was something he couldn't endure. He was only sixteen when a pair of broncs he was driving as lead team didn't start out well, and the owner began striking them. A D dropped the lines on the roll, got off on the far side, and walked away. He was nearly ten rods away before the man saw him. "Where you goin'?" he demanded. A D didn't stop. "Go to hell!" he yelled back. The owner kept stalling for three days, refusing to give A D his time, but finally had to give in.

Bob Dahl also came to the woods at sixteen, a scared green kid straight from North Dakota. The boss assumed he could handle horses, and Bob, not daring to admit his inexperience for fear he'd lose the job, learned by watching others. He had only one close shave. A teamster ahead of him spilled a load going down a bank, and didn't clean it up— a flagrant disregard of the unwritten law. Bob was even afraid to report it, and cleaned it up himself. He finished the season as a full-fledged teamster.

Though he was a shell-shocked victim of World War I, moody and at times unapproachable, Art Hegdahl was an excellent teamster. He had a strawberry roan horse that was a killer, and a big sorrel that was balky, which no one but Art seemed able to handle. The other teamsters gave these two horses a wide berth, not wanting to go near them. But Art spent hours in the barn after everyone else left, tending them. He had a way of talking and whispering to them that tamed them, and mastered their behavior.

When his troubles closed in on him, he'd go to town and get drinking. Generally he would bring back a bottle which he kept hid among the feed sacks in the barn. One night, when someone heard him in the barn apparently talking to the animals, they took a closer look. And then looked again. Art was on his knees, under the belly of the killer horse, currying it and petting it, talking all the while, as the horse stood tamely as a kitten.

Balky horses needed special handling. There was a rumor that such horses could be started by pouring a cupful of water in each ear, which sounded like a most inhumane practice. It was said that before you tried it, you'd better be ready to travel: when the horse finally felt the effect of it, he would take off like a rocket.

Supplying horses for camps was a job in itself. At one point, Leonard Dickinson had seventy-six horses on Ile Royale and Grand Marais. They were brought to Ile Royale on barges, and swum ashore. Horses rented for twenty-five dollars a month, per team, in 1930; but this was a hard job, with deep snow, in rocky country, and the horses earned every bit.

Knowing how to handle horses gave a man pride and confidence. He was an expert, and he knew it. When Liver Lip Hoover was jobhunting, he was asked what he could do. To Liver Lip, that was a stupid question. "Can't you tell a four-horse teamster?" he growled. "A man with a high-crowned hat, stag pants, and low shoes—he *always* drives horses!" He could or would do little else. When the four-horse-team era ended, old Hoover was relegated to hanging around saloons, spearing drinks. From there he slid backwards to being a swamper in Dutch Mary's place, where he waddled around keeping the fires. Mary said he wasn't good for anything else, and Mary should have known. But as a teamster, he'd had his moment of glory.

One complication of hauling was that the most direct route very often led through swamps and over unbridged creeks. These could never be crossed in summer. It was possible in winter, to get a road surface that would support the heavy loads, by freezing it. Country dwellers who fear for their septic tanks in winter will understand how this was possible. A small crew, with cat to compact the surface and insure hard freezing, usually created a winter hauling road that cut many weary miles off the hauling.

It was miserable. By its very nature, it had to be done at the coldest time of winter. We were seven miles cross-country from civilization when Earl Peloquin, on Coon Creek, went through the ice up to his chin. We were stretching our work day to its outermost limits, so it was nearly dark at the time; we quit immediately and started walking him back to town, but with the thermometer at a minus 30 degrees his clothing soon froze so stiffly he was almost immobilized. We had to put his arms across our shoulders and half-drag him to the antifreeze station, where after we had a few stiff ones he felt capable of going another half-mile home to bed in his wet clothes. When I timed my own cold bath in the same creek at 10 A.M. a day or so later, Harry Morse stripped off his long johns, and I wore them while he wore his outer Sioux-wools without under-clothing, while mine were dried over a fire. It was a high-priority job, so we didn't waste time going back to camp.

Power was needed to move the big sleigh loads of logs. Oxen got the job done. When an ox got hurt or old, he often ended up in camp stew. (Itasca County Historical Society)

Truckers showed the same urgency about getting the hauling done. The few side track places that allowed for passing weren't always at the right place; sometimes the roar of his own truck prevented a driver from hearing a load approach in time for him to duck into one. At such times, the loaded truck had the right of way. Vern Skallman was coming back to camp hell-for-leather, intent on getting reloaded and back on another trip, when he saw another truck howling down the grade, bearing down on him. To meet head on was death to both. Without hesitation Vern plowed into the timber at the side of the road, banging and bouncing down a ravine. How he lived to tell about it is a miracle.

One year there was some debate about crossing a small lake that obstructed the most direct route to town. I said the ice was unsafe; Bill, having measured it, proclaimed that army engineers would certify it as strong enough to carry a railroad locomotive, and the truck driver agreed with him. He didn't, however, want to make the trip alone, so against my better judgment I was drafted to accompany him. But I laid down one stipulation: we would keep our doors open, and I would watch the load constantly; if I shouted, "Jump!" we must both leap out of the truck without hesitating a second. He agreed, somewhat scornfully.

It seemed at first as if I had been chicken for nothing; the truck rolled slowly but steadily over the crackling frozen surface. We were perhaps a half mile from shore when we heard the CRACK! that meant business, simultaneously I saw the trailer wheels dig in and water rise under them. I yelled "Jump!" and catapulted myself sixteen feet over the ice. The driver was a split second slower, and landed on his hands and knees just as the doors shut with a bang and the truck dropped thru the ice.

We had saved ourselves, but there was the man's brand-new truck and a load of pulp.

It took the better part of three days of flaring tempers, Herculean effort and a conglomeration of riggin', equipment crew and spectators, before we got the truck and load out, but we suffered only a needless expense and (on my part) an unexpected cold bath in the lake when I fell in during the frenzied activity. But the whole thing was needless: we never used that route, even when the ice grew sound.

LOADING LOGS WITH HORSES
AND CROSS HAUL

6

Getting Out the Timber

Babe pulled the water tank to ice the roads for Paul's winter logging. One day it sprang a leak, and the water ran out, all the way down to New Orleans, and that's how the Mississippi River was formed. Babe was real temperamental—he wouldn't haul loads unless there was snow. So Paul fooled him—he whitewashed the roads.

Horses not only figured in hauling out the timber; they formed the supply-line that kept the camps in operation. The outside world was reached by a supply road called the "tote road" over which a lone teamster would travel to some outpost of civilization (usually reached by a railroad) to pick up the beef quarters, flour, beans, coffee, and other staples, oats for the horses, the mail, and the Copenhagen snuff, which kept the jacks going.

It was an all-weather-travel job, over long, improvised roads that were mostly bad, with the task of loading and unloading at the ends of the journey. In summer the tote teamster used a wagon, in winter a sleigh, and his well-being was his own problem.

The Keewatin and Namakan camps got supplies from Bovey and Grand Rapids, and Ed Carlson drove tote teams for them, over the fifty-mile distance. That meant two or three days on the lonely woods trails, depending on road conditions and the size of his load. Usually he could plan to stop one night at the Smith house near Balsam. Then a long day's travel took him deep in the wilderness, where he would camp that night, after feeding and blanketing his horses. He would crawl into his bed roll fully clothed, fur parka and all, in a nest in the hay to keep warm.

For protection he carried a rifle, and was constantly on guard for the timber wolves which followed his sleigh, attracted by the smell of either meat or horseflesh. Though he kept a good fire going in the evening, he said, the wolves sometimes tried to attack the horses. They would gather in the darkness, in a ring outside the firelight, and charge, trying to bite the horses' legs. When they did, the horses would lash out with their hind hoofs, and unlucky wolves would go flying with a screaming howl.

Ed shot several wolves on those trips. Nights in the wild were always a time of anxiety as he tried to protect the horses and himself from hungry attackers. Many times he prayed, asking that the wolves go away so that he and the horses could rest.

Since tote roads were little more than forest trails, it was not unusual to meet wild animals.

Art Barrett, while traveling at night, encountered a bear. He had a moment's warning when his little dog gave the alarm, barking furiously. The bear retaliated by leaping at the dog, and the dog promptly ducked behind his master for protection. The only weapon Barrett had was a twelve-gauge shotgun, with a faulty firing pin so that it didn't always fire when the trigger was pulled. Still, it was his only weapon, so he shoved it out. The bear stood up and seized the gun by the barrel, trying to wrest it away. His heart in his mouth, Barrett pulled the trigger, and his luck held—the gun went off, blowing the bear's head to bits. The force of the charge knocked Barrett backwards.

Hay for the horses was hauled from the wild meadows, where it had been cut and stacked in the summer. The loading operation usually required two men, to secure the load with binding poles. Frank Werthner worked with Ed Carlson on that job, hauling with two teams to Quinn's Camp, near Pickerel Lake. They were told to "keep the camp in hay," and left to work out the "how" of it themselves.

It was a twelve-mile haul, and required two days, what with loading and unloading, and an overnight stay at Deer Creek Farm Camp. It worked like an assembly line, and in a week's time they had transferred a mountain of hay.

But Ed, an old "company" man, wasn't satisfied. He said, "We ought to do it in one day."

Frank wasn't quite so enthused. He pointed out that this would involve leaving camp in the wee dark hours, and returning at midnight, and he wanted no part of it. So that was that.

Then came trouble. Coming down Shine Lake hill on the narrow road, with big loads on narrow-gauge sleighs, was treacherous, and Ed's sleigh, following Frank's, slid sidewise and tipped over. They were forced to slip the binding pole, unload, take the sleigh to the foot of the hill, reload, and continue. It was eleven o'clock before they reached the camp, and another hour before they could leave their teams.

They had of course missed supper, but cooks always left lunch and a big coffee pot of scalding brew. Frank was ready to turn in, but not Ed. "We gotta unload, so we can get going in the morning," he urged. Frank refused—so Ed went out and unloaded alone, working all night.

That did it. Frank had had enough. As far as he was concerned, Ed was beyond reason. He quit the hauling, and from then on, Ed toted hay by himself.

Times of strain might call for high production and longer hauls, by the tote teams, but long trips were hard on the horses. Making the twenty-three mile jaunt to Bigfork for supplies was considered a two-day trip. When an ambitious teamster did it in one day, the poor horses were so tired, Frank said, they could hardly walk.

Long after the sleigh haul had given way to the truck, horses continued to be used in the woods, for skidding.

Skidding was an art of its own. Basically, it was the movement of timber from the woods where it had been fallen, either by dragging the logs on the ground with chain or tongs, or by hauling on loaded drays. It was moved to a skidway or landing area along the logging road, from where it was loaded and hauled out.

Short skidding of logs was done directly on the ground. Skidding tongs were used on bigger logs, but chains bound several logs together where the timber was small. Once the skidding trail was broken into the snow, and frozen, the logs slid along easily. Longer skidding drays were used. Larger loads could be hauled. Some skidding drays were called "go-devils" or "jumpers," designed to get over and avoid stumps.

The skidding of short timber, such as ties, eight-foot pulpwood, and posts was done on four-foot wide double-bunk drays with four foot high stakes. The teams could easily handle a single cord.

Gyppo-skidding, a good man could get out fifteen cords a day, working alone. Two men with a team upped that to twenty or twenty-five cords, and two men with two teams, working together, could get it up to fifty.

"Hot logging" was a method of logging that saved one handling of the logs. As they were skidded out to the landings, they were loaded onto the sleighs. But it was often hard to coordinate this system; usually the logs were skidded and "cold decked" at the skidways or landings early in the fall. Sleigh hauling commenced later, in December, when snow and frost helped make the roads support the heavy sleighs.

In practice, skidding required close cooperation between man and beast, maneuvering around the stump. Rough terrain created special problems.

One job I recall that developed certain special techniques was at the beginning of World War II, when we had an urgent order of mining and trestle timber to get out for United States Steel's Oliver Mining Company division. With President Roosevelt making his weekly pleas in his fireside chats for all-out war production, Mr. Leonards, the head of Oliver Mining Company, promised us top priority on any equipment or men we might need. Ships to keep the war effort going could not be built without iron, and without timber, the mines couldn't operate.

That winter we had four or five feet of snow in the woods. The hills were so steep in places the horses could barely get up them, let alone come down with a load—the logs would run over them. We decided that the only solution was to have my brother Sam (a wizard with the cat) make side-hill trails like switchbacks in packed snow, and have the teams skid to the cat trail. From there the cat could take a big drag of logs to the landing. In order to make best use of big landings for sorting and loading the timber we picked a large flat grassy slough. This would become an impossible wet quagmire in summer; we had to get the timber off those hills before spring.

Even so, we had a problem. The trails facing south got icy, and horses had to be well shod, or they could lose their footing and get hurt. The long piling gave no trouble—they were fine to skid. But often the short, smooth Norway pine logs would take off and slide into the horses.

Billy Goheen, whom I'd sometimes have to work on the steepest pitches because he seemed most capable of handling the horses and still getting the timber out, never complained.

Billy was quite elderly when I met him, in 1940. He was a fine old gentleman and just as fine a teamster. He wore a medium brim hat with full crown over a silk stocking all winter. Though not much for small talk, Billy said to me, "Me boy, I niver thought we'd be able to work the horses on these steep hills and get this timber out. But those cat trails sure saved the horses. We'll make 'er now."

Whenever my supervisory chores were caught up, I enjoyed pitching in to help with the work. I helped him skid often, swinging eveners and setting chains or tongs, appreciating his ability to get the horses to respond with the least words. The horses knew, too, for he always got the timber out the right way, making it easy for them.

One day he said, "Me boy, if ye'll get some extra chains, we'll get those pesky small logs out easier, by trailing three sets of logs behind each other."

I got the chains, and, sure enough, by chaining the logs in three sets of two logs each, the weight and drag would prevent them from sliding ahead into the horses. We singled the horses on small logs as much as possible, thereby resting them a half-day at a time.

We had five teams skidding on this job, and one team cross-hauling at the jammer. But the teamsters were not all like Mr. Goheen. They were good teamsters, but some problems develop among men that cannot be resolved. The steep hills and deep snow didn't help matters, and the tempers of some men got on edge.

At any rate, the day I picked up two teamsters in Craig, the lumberjack hangout in those days, I didn't have much choice. I needed them, and three or four cutters, so I just took what was available. As I drove to camp in my brother Bill's nine-passenger Packard, I noticed the two teamsters, Jack and Bozo, scrapping in the back of the car. I stopped and asked what the problem was, but they just muttered. I invited everyone out for a little stretch, then asked if anybody had a drink. Several men fished out bottles from packs. I said, "We'll drink 'er up, boys; we can't bring any of this stuff to camp."

PULP HOOK

One day shortly thereafter, I observed from a distance the teamster Jack about to take off with his team and load down a fairly steep chute, with several long piling. He called his signal, and started down. Further down the hill was Bozo, stubborn and quarrelsome as ever. There was no doubt he heard the signal, and had time to wait as Jack's team came down at a fast trot, but he snatched up his lines in a hurry after making his hitch, and started. He would be crossing in front of the other team where the trails joined.

Jack couldn't stop, once he had started, and he hollered for Bozo to hold back. But Bozo kept going. Jack's team pushed right over Bozo's, and one of Bozo's horses went down.

I got there as fast as I could run. The two teamsters were squaring off at each other, about to fight. "Cut it out!" I yelled. "Let's get these horses untangled so we can get that horse up."

Jack turned to help me unbuckle the harness, while Bozo stood and glared. I glanced back just in time to see Bozo move to take a swing at Jack, and hollered at him again; then he turned on me. I said, "Beat it, before you get into trouble." Bozo took off for camp, swearing, picked up his check, and left.

After Jack and I got the horses untangled and back on their feet, I drove the team, which seemed none the worse, for the rest of the day. Next day I put a spare cutter to driving them, and we had no further trouble. I never did hear what caused the friction between the two teamsters.

Not all teamsters resorted to fights and swearing. Hadley Malvig was a different sort of man altogether. His horses got so well-trained they could even travel on their own between the woods and the landing, if the trail was without obstruction, with the lines tied up on the hames and tongs holding the logs. But one time, while he was swamping out logs, the horses got extra confident and took off on their own before he'd hitched them to the logs. Hadley was alarmed, when he saw they'd gone, fearing that the second horse would step into the sharp tongs of the lead horse on the trail, and injure himself. A Christian believer, Hadley knew where to turn for help. As he ran for the landing, he prayed that the horses would not be hurt. His prayer was answered: when he arrived, breathless, the horses were safe—the landing man had caught and tied them.

Some horses developed uncanny tricks for getting rid of the loads on drays, even though sharp spikes were driven into the bunks to hold the load in place. In rough going, over low stumps or small hummocks, the dray load would sway sideways, then pitch forward, running into a rock or stump. One good teamster, George Volk, had an ornery team of wild hay-burners. They were known to be notorious runaways, but George handled them without mishap. One clever little trick they liked to use was to give a little jerk or bunt in starting the load after each stop. Every time they did, the load would shift back, until it overbalanced and slid off and had to be reloaded. They went through this little performance until George got a sharp stick and used it as a prod every time the team would bunt. At the same time, we put chain binders on the loads for him. It seemed to cure his problem.

Skidding and cutting had to be coordinated for most efficiency. Matt Strom worked for Frank Werthner one fall, cutting balsam and spruce logs for Reid's mill. Matt, being a highball woodsman, cut fast and furiously until he had logs piled four to six feet high all over the woods. But Frank wasn't a bit happy over the high production. His one team couldn't keep up with the skidding, much less the hauling. He had to hire another team to get his logs out before snow covered them.

"Original" is a term for a horse that can be dangerous, or even a killer. Such horses are to be regarded with great caution; no man should ever let himself be caught or cornered by one. The condition results from the gelding of a high-strung young stallion: during castration, one testicle may get hung up so it is not extracted. The horse becomes frustrated and unruly.

We had obtained such a horse from a dealer. Though he was a good horse, and beautiful (a deep maroon color), he showed fiery red color in his eyes. He wasn't safe for an ordinary man to handle, but with a good master, he could be worked.

Two bachelor brothers who were small loggers saw the horse, and fell in love with him. They begged to buy him. We were reluctant, and explained the problem, but they were undeterred. They liked the horse, they could handle him, they said, and took him to camp. They worked him for some time, pleased and happy with him. Everything seemed fine.

Returning home from a trip to town, all in good order, the brothers separated, one to prepare a meal while the other tended the horses in the barn. But the brother in the barn did not come in for his supper, and the other got uneasy. He went to look, and found his brother trampled to death under the horse.

Gust Edstrom entertained us often with tall tales of his miraculous wild and original horses. A witty, highly intelligent fellow, he was over-qualified for woods work, or most anything else in the common run. Counselors at the Veterans Hospital were greatly impressed with his intellect, and spoke seriously of the high position he ought to aspire to. Gust thereupon offered to fill the vacancy created at that time by the resignation of Vice-President Agnew, but nothing came of it.

Len Knotts is probably the granddaddy of all skidders. He has the unusual distinction of having started with oxen, graduated to horses, then being converted to the mechanized cats and at last the rubber tired skidders. He claims to have skidded more timber than any man in Minnesota. He also has the record of having the longest active career of any lumberjack now living in the Bigfork Valley.

Teamsters got top pay, but they didn't get rich. Before Christmas in 1921, a time when wages were quite good, four-horse teamsters were paid about seventy dollars per month, two-horse teamsters fifty dollars, and swampers forty dollars. But a sudden depression hit with the new year, and wages dropped to half. The work schedule, however, remained the same.

Driving horses in the woods was always interesting, and crammed with action. The movement of the timber out of the woods depended wholly on the ability of the men and horses to do the job. Skilled, steadfast, resourceful and reliable men did the job.

Visitors as well as those who were involved in the work enjoyed watching the ever-fascinating activity, as men and teams skidded and loaded logs out of the woods, and teams hauled the big groaning sleighs down the roads. Tripping the loads over the river bank landing, with the rolling logs crashing and booming, the sounds echoing off into the distance are an indelible memory to anyone who was ever a part of it.

Toploading was the liveliest activity in the woods. The toploader was "top dog," alert, nimble, and skillful, and clever as a cat on his feet. He had to be prepared to make lightning decisions as the logs came up on a parbuckle, and the "senders" had to know their business as well, to prevent the large end of the log gaining, or the log going up "catty-wampus." Imagine a ton-and-a-half lunker coming at you on the end of a rope sling, while you're standing on a pile of other logs armed only with peavey, and you get the idea. You'd better be clawing for the sky. A good way to train for the job would be to practice the Highland fling while standing on a pile of potatoes.

Agility was only part of it. The toploader had to "know his onions" when it came to logs. It was imperative that he fit logs properly in building up a sleigh load; otherwise, should a sudden shift or movement take place in the sleigh haul, the load would be "sluiced," or spilled on the road. That meant moving the timber out of the way so as not to stop the next load coming down the road, and then reloading it. No self-respecting top-loader allowed that to happen.

**TIE BUCKER'S
SHOULDER PAD**

**CAT'S PAW OR
CHAIN BITE**

To keep sleighs from being "rocker bound," they were loaded at a level spot.

The job called for teamwork between the hookers, or "senders," the cross-haul teamster, and the top-loader. Sturdy hardwood skids were notched to fit against the rockers of the sleigh on an incline, or the side of the load as it built up. A loading line, or long chain, was wrapped around the log on the skidway with a parbuckle or swamp hook fastened to one end. This hook was first fastened back to a stump or tree on the loading side of the sleigh.

The top-loader called the shots, signalling "go-ahead" to the teamster guiding his team steadily forward. The log was rolled up onto the rockers or bunks of the sleigh, and secured on the opposite side of the sleigh rockers with cornerbind chains. Sometimes two logs were fastened in the cornerbinds, making a firm lock to the outboard logs. Logs for the next tier were brought up until the rockers were filled to the near side, closest to the skidway. The last log which filled out the first tier was placed on the rocker, and likewise cinched with the cornerbind chains.

Then started the "tricks" of the toploader, or "skyhooker," of "walling up;" building up straight side walls to his load of round logs. He must choose certain well-fitting logs to lie on top of others on the outside walls. The off side was called the "Canadian side." The tiers of logs were brought over to the offside, and filled in, back to the near side.

The top-loader would call for certain size logs to fit his "jigsaw puzzle," and a certain number of wraps would deliver the log to the spot he chose. The parbuckle hook was driven into the log near that spot. The senders with canthooks or peavies would "cut" or steer the log so the big end would not gain too fast as the log went up the skids. The top-loader called "Hi!" to the teamster, who stopped the team immediately on that command. If he went a bit too far, it could be disastrous to the top-loader and his logs; like a basket of eggs they could spill over. The top-loader's work was swift and sure with the log in motion. He could pinch it over, or snub it to stop it in the right place.

To remove the chain from under a log, the signal "chain" was called to the teamster.

Rising two or three tiers of logs on the side walls, chocking blocks were used to hold the logs in position. Wrapping chains were next thrown loosely around the load. Then they would fill the "basket." When the load reached the desired height, another set of wrappers was run over the load. The pressure of logs over these wrappers bound the load tightly together. Logs piled above this were called "rounding 'er up." The top logs, sometimes called the "Canadian peaks," brought the load to a balance. The top-loader would check, standing on top and rocking the load. If it was balanced, the saying was, "she's on the pin."

Without exception, top-loaders were cool, confident men, daring but not reckless. It was as much as their life was worth to get careless—a big log falling back or flipping over too far could kill a man or maim him for life. Leaping and skipping out of the way went with the job, along with handling a canthook or peavey with utmost dexterity.

Disaster nearly overtook one man toploading his own load, when he lost his balance while trying to pry a bundle of small logs into place. He fell to the ground, with the logs tumbling after him. But miracle of miracles, the horses hadn't slacked off and the ground men hadn't tripped the crotch chains. The bundle stopped a scant eighteen inches above the fallen man. Needless to say, the crew scrambled to get him out of there in a hurry.

I saw what happened when one man went out on the job before breakfast one day, and fortified himself with a chaw of tobacco from time to time to still the pangs of hunger. The load was nearing the peak when the force of a giant sneeze catapulted him off to the ground. He broke his nose, his jaw, some teeth, and was generally banged up, but the worst was he had to take a lot of ribbing after that.

Other methods of loading developed that were easier for the top-loader, and much faster. The side jammer came into being in the early 1900s. This was built of two heavy base timbers or runners, with cross-beams fastened to the base. On one set of runners, two long lead timbers, forty-foot spruce or Norway, were fastened with iron straps shaped into heavy hinges, pinning the leads and runner together. The leads were fastened together in an "A" form at the top with "bale and bolt," from which a pulley was hung. From the top of the leads to the opposite runner, two wooden squared poles were fastened within an iron slide bracket. The bracket had holes, as well as the top sliding pole, called the "reach." The latter affair was to hold the leads up when tipped slightly back and not in use, or while moving it to the next skidway.

To the top of the leads were fastened two guy lines, cable-secured to stumps or trees, that held the jammer leads when tilted over the center of the load for loading.

A long cable was used, running from the loading end, where a pair of crotch chains were fastened to logs with end hooks and ropes, for the hookers to guide the log as it went up. The cable then went up over the top pulley and down to the base, where another pulley was fastened. The line ran out to a convenient distance for hitching a team of horses to a chain on the end of the cable. This was a directline pull for the team.

When lifting heavy logs, another pulley was attached to the log-lifting end of the cable, called a running block. This hook-up gave double purchasing power to the team.

After cutting the necessary timbers, my father and I built one of these jammers in one day. I'm sure he'd built many before, and we built many after that. Later we built several swing-boom jammers, more complex affairs, excellent for use in loading pulpwood as well as logs. My brother Norman built the first truck-mounted power jammer, on an old 1924 White truck. Called "Popeye," that jammer gave excellent service for years.

A method similar to the side jammer was a "gin pole" or "stiff leg." This was simply an upright timber rigged like a side jammer, and served the same purpose.

I even saw one outfit using a leaning tree rigged for loading logs. It seemed to work okay.

Another simple method was to find a place on a hillside for a skidway. The sleigh was placed just below the skidway, and the logs rolled on. But it wasn't always possible to find such a place conveniently located, nor could they load as high loads.

One spring, Len Knotts was loading big pulp sticks that had been left behind when hand loading, due to their size. The men were tired, and when one big brute was raised three times, only to slide back to the ground when it was nearly on the truck, Len gave up. He said to the boss, "How much will you take for that stick? I'll pay for it, and you can leave the s.o.b. right here."

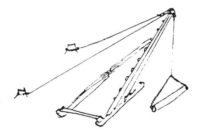

SIDE JAMMER FOR LOADING LOGS

A horrible fate befell one toploader I knew. Broken-Ass Ole was a nimble little fellow with a fund of dry humor. You could recognize him some distance off by his hurry-up gait and his hunched, bent-over stance. It always seemed that his head was intent on getting there faster than his feet could make it. He came by his name and his posture in the line of duty. Toploaders customarily dismounted when the load was topped out, after first shipping their peavey, by slipping down with a hand on the wrapper chain, or, in more flamboyant cases, just leaping off the load. Ole used this second style—but in one unfortunate instance he miscalculated, or slipped on takeoff. Whatever the cause, he landed seat first on the upright handle of the peavey. It hurts just to think about it, so it's not hard to imagine what it did to Ole.

George Scanlon, an old top-loader whose later life was spent along skid row, was frequently in need of money after a drunk. After one such bout, sleeping it off in the woods, he bethought himself of a means to earn a much-needed drink. He gathered rotten log material, dried it, and crushed it to a powder. This he packaged, and sold for "bedbug powder," hawking it door-to-door in Grand Rapids. It must have been a needed commodity, for he sold the powder to nearly every household he approached, and made enough to buy the drinks he badly needed.

One thing can be said for the methods of loading and hauling. They were the most efficient way known to the men in their time, made from simple materials on hand, while handling tremendous volumes of goods. Necessity was truly the mother of invention.

Steam haulers were ugly, cumbersome monsters, but they could outdistance the horses on the long sleigh hauls. They towed trains of eight to twelve sleighs, and could travel over rough terrain and up grades where horses could not work.

The steam hauler seems to have come from Maine, with the "Lombard," in 1901, being first, but there are reports of others in early Minnesota use. The Maine ones were piloted by a horse in a pair of shafts attached in front of the engine. It must have been a comedy to see the puffing, chattering, track-laying freak followed by a train of huge loaded sleighs, the whole being led by a horse. This creation was the great-granddaddy of the modern Caterpillar.

In the Bigfork area, they first saw service in the Erskine Brothers' camps of the early twenties. Al Hanson drove a ten-ton Holt, pulling six sleighs in one train, and five on his next trip, with three sets of sleighs being needed: one on the road, one being loaded, and one being unloaded. According to Zade Cochran, the scaler, they hauled 44,000 board feet of pine logs per train load.

Loading was adjusted somewhat, with the rear sleighs on the train being loaded progressively lighter so as not to put too great a strain on the tongues, hitches, and bunting poles connecting the train. Two trips on the nine-mile haul meant long days, so Al, already known as "Cat" Hanson, picked up the name "Moonlight."

The old method of starting sleighs with a maul was useless in these circumstances. It was necessary to back up to get slack, then bunt ahead to break the runners loose, and Hanson would jerk the cat back and forth to get the train moving. Sometimes this ripping and snorting would break the hitches, which in its turn resulted in many an outburst of temper on a cold morning. Hanson acquired still another name: "Bulldog."

Speed was essential in loading, as well, to keep up with "Moonlight" running five or six loads with each trip of the cat train. Hadley Malvig, driving crosshaul team, said that a "loading bar" made for a quick trip of the logs when the top-loader called out "Hi!" With a good, lively team, they could keep up with "Bulldog" easily. Long before daylight they could hear the cat engine, pounding and roaring as it clawed its way on the frozen snow, pulling the groaning sleighs.

Presently there was another cat on the job, a "Best," which must have seen service elsewhere, as it had "City of Hibbing" painted on its cab. A man named Schwartz learned to drive it, spotting sleighs and making up trains in the woods.

Erskine Brothers went west in 1926, but "Mad Cat" Hanson stuck with the cats. He bought the cats, sleighs, and rigging, and contracted for a twelve-mile sleigh haul from Zaiser's camp in the Kondike Rocks. They ran the cat two shifts, pulling ten or twelve sleighs—Schwartz on days, Hanson nights, never stopping more than necessary for fuel and grease. They carried extra parts and buckets of bolts to make emergency repairs on the fly, for Hanson was determined that the cat would make the trip, no matter what.

Since it took the driver's full attention just to navigate, a conductor-brakeman was needed to watchdog the loads and keep the sleighs tracking. My brother Art took this on, when he was nineteen. His job was to jump from sleigh to sleigh, adjust the crotch chains when there was slack on the turns, and see that the binding chains held the loads tight so that they didn't shift. Lunch had to be eaten on a catch-as-catch-can basis. "Moonlight" was opposed to any coddling of menials, so Art had to gulp his lunch down on the back sleighs, meanwhile swinging his lantern to show that all was well. If Al didn't constantly see Art's lantern, he would stop the train and come back, cussing.

One night when the thermometer stuck at forty below and the mercury went out of sight, the train was dragging hard on the snow road, with the engine burning up gas faster than usual. It was plain that they would run out before their half-way fueling stop. Al told Art, "You get off and run to the Baker place, fill up two five-gallon cans with gas and run back to the Coon Creek bridge, and pour in the gas on the fly. I'm running out of gas, and we won't make the hill."

Art took off running several miles to the gas stop, and returned with the cans—not full, however, because he couldn't carry that much gas and run fast enough. He gassed the cat as it labored up the grade, but it was already running out of power. Al, his chin stuck out hard, was frantically shifting into lower gears, but it finally stuck, halfway up the incline. Then he began backing the sleighs to get slack, jerking, and trying to bunt the sleighs for a new start.

Things went from bad to worse. He tore the tongue hitch nut of the first sleigh. By this time he had chewed up the hill, getting the sleigh out of line so he could get hooked up to the rest of the train. The air was blue from his cussing madness.

Art could see that bull force wasn't accomplishing anything. He suggested, "Why don't you take half the train over at a time?"

Bulldog growled, "What the hell do you know about driving cat, kid?"

Art never said another word, watching while Hanson continued chewing dirt in the ruts up the hill. They finally made it by unhooking the sleighs, dragging them up one at a time. This took so much time they didn't get back to camp until noon the next day, and it cost the day crew their turn.

Patience was not Hanson's long suit. One very cold night the cat stopped, out in the middle of the bog. "Crank it," he told Art. Art cranked until he was tired. Then Al came and cranked. It just wouldn't start.

By this time Art, holding the lantern, had noticed frost around the carburetor and gas line. He suggested to Al that that might be the cause of the trouble.

Bulldog snarled, "What the hell do you know about cat engines, kid?" But after another round of fruitless cranking, he decided to remove the carburetor. Sure enough, there was ice. By this time his fingers were so cold that his temper was wild, and he heaved the offending carburetor out in the woods. Then he ordered Art to resume cranking.

Art told him what anyone should have known—it would never run without the carburetor. But Bulldog wasn't ready to accept any advice. There were more bitter words, and Art decided it was hopeless. He started down the road for camp.

Al ran after him. "Where'n hell do you think you're going?"

Art said, "Somewhere else to work," and kept on walking. Al took a swing at him, but Art was quicker, and warned him not to try again. Bulldog then changed his tune, and begged Art to come back, help him find the carburetor, and try once more.

"Not unless you promise not to swear at me, and to quit treating me like some dumb kid," Art said. "You behave like a reasonable man from now on, or it's no go."

Bulldog was still fuming mad at the end, but he promised. Art found the carburetor, they built a fire, thawed it, installed it, gave the engine a crank—and it took right off.

Al Hanson was true to his word. He and Art never again had a cross word, though they worked together the rest of the winter, and eventually became lifelong friends.

A D Moors was another early cat-skinner in the Bigfork country. He learned on the ten-ton Holt owned by the county. The regular driver was Claus Swanson, an old man who disliked the jolting and bouncing that went with the stump-pulling job. "Come on up and drive," he coaxed A D, and showed him all the control levers. Before the day was out, A D had the hang of it, and it became his job. For years that cat was used on roads in winter, pushing a big V-snowplow with wing plows operated by hand chain hoists. Unwieldy as it was, it was a sight to make men marvel and kids all over the country long for the day when they might be in the catbird seat of the rumbling chattering mountainous thing.

In the camps, however, the cat's main purpose was the sleigh haul. On the Galvin Line A D hauled twelve sleighs, four trips a day on a five-mile iced road. The sleighs were big bruisers, with eight-foot runner spread and sixteen-foot rockers, that hauled 5,000 to 7,000 board feet of logs per sleigh. Together with another cat train, they were putting in over a quarter-million board feet of pine per day.

A D also had a session with "Mad Cat" Hanson. As he was climbing a long grade, with the sleighs dragging heavily, the cat began to slow down. Bulldog waved his arms, signalling "go faster," but A D ignored him—it was all he could do to hang in there and hope the cat would make the hill. It did, and near the top, Bulldog ran up and jumped on the cat, yelling," "Why didn't you go faster?"

A D, a peppery little Irishman himself, yelled back, "This damn thing has got only one speed, and that's slow. If you want it to go faster, drive it yourself."

Hanson jumped off and never said another word about it.

Everyone seemed to realize that Hanson's bursts of temper were caused by his frenzied desire to have high production. He never spared himself, staying up day and night fixing the monsters when they broke down. Many nights it was said Bulldog got in at 3:00 A.M., leaned back in the office chair, pulled his Scotch cap over his eyes, and dozed off for an hour, never even turning the light off. He tried to cram more work into one lifetime than many would get in a dozen.

For all that, apparently his abrasive temper got him in bad with some company stooges, and for awhile he was in disfavor. He went to selling the "Caterpillar," a new machine modeled after the Holt and the Best. This famous machine changed the landscape all over the world. Others like it came out in the thirties—International TracTractor, Cletrac, Allis Chalmers. Through the years they continued to improve.

Our first "cat" was an International TracTractor, a good machine in its time, with a hydraulic angled bulldozer blade. My brothers Hubert and Sam became experts with it, making roads and clearing land. Eventually that cat took part in the building of the AlCan Highway, where it was finally worn out and pushed into the road fill near Ft. St. John. In a manner of speaking, it's still on the job.

As for Moonlight, he was soon reinstated in the company as walking boss over gyppo loggers. A few years of that, and he went back to join the crowd of loggers himself.

Al Hanson deserves a lot of credit for his vision, leadership and hard determination. He had fresh new ideas, and was willing to tackle many things that looked impossible to other men. Among loggers, he rates another tribute: he moved more timber out of the woods with cats and trucks in those days than his competitors in the game. He was likeable in spite of his short temper. Right or wrong, he took many risks on his own, and never really asked a man to do anything he wouldn't attempt himself.

Another point is that he retired more horses from the horse-killing phases of skidding and hauling. The cat brought an end to the era that glorified horses as beasts of burden with nearly the same status in the camps as the men. But, looking back on all this (and I'm sure many others feel the same way) I believe we'd be better off with horses doing much of the timber skidding out of the woods. With the cost of machinery skyrocketing and the energy crisis, future generations of loggers may come back to horseflesh. Properly handled, they can do a lot of work. Their feed can be raised on a small acreage of land, so the energy cost is little more than some work. But—find a good harness-maker before attempting to change back.

Regardless of modern efficiency, it seems that men with horses moved more timber out of the woods than has been done in any other way, since logging began in Minnesota.

Another piece of automotive machinery helped push the horse off the road and changed his status from that of working partner to the position of pet. That was the motor truck.

With the disappearance of river log driving and the logging railroad, a new way had to be developed to get the timber to the mills, and the motor truck came into its own. First came Dan Burman with his 1925 Dodge, and Pete Phillips with his exciting-sounding Reo Speedwagon. Towering Harry Lamson, the biggest man in the north country, had a truck which was already loaded when he climbed into the cab; and Carl Peterson was the fourth of the pioneer truckers. They ground up and down the impossible hills with old-model trucks barely able to churn their way up with a load, probably costing as much in gas and parts as they earned. But it was the only way left to go—the railroad was gone.

It was a young man's game, calling for quick reactions, and familiarity with the quirks of the gasoline engine. They were the daring young men over whom the girls swooned and the bosses gloated. It took consummate skill to be able to back and turn a truck and trailer in the space where a normal man would hesitate to turn a car. They did it and thought nothing of it. "Nor snow, nor rain, nor gloom of night" ever stopped the truck drivers from jockeying their twelve-ton loads on one and one-half-ton trucks out of the swamps and over the hills of the poorly graded roads.

Sid Williams, of the old school, looked upon these gay blades with a jaundiced eye. "All them damn young punks know is to goose 'em, double-clutch 'em, and blow the horn," he snorted. But this was far from true.

Lyndon Kendall was considered King of the Road. George Lund became a master in putting together truck routes, and came with a fleet. The trucks couldn't stand the punishment of the rough roads and power demands, and he traded the darned things off almost as soon as the down payment was used up; the old finance man, Saxhaug, told me it really kept him jumping.

Highway No. 38 to Grand Rapids was the truck driver's nightmare. It was a looping, narrow, roller-coaster winding on narrow hog's backs past lakes and up steep hills that rose one after another with no level stretch to make a run at it. Even today, there are just about three places where there's a decent chance to overtake and pass another vehicle. The test was "Stake Hill" on the Continental Divide, named for the impressive number of guard stakes on its narrow shoulder. Coming up over glare ice, the lack of power slowed the load and forced the driver to double-clutch 'er and shift 'er into the "beanhole," super-low. He had to shoot it in with smooth motion, not letting the engine lurch or the wheels spin. If he didn't make it, he went back over the drop-off, thirty feet, and it was goodbye truck and driver, too. The only driver I know of who slid down and ever drove again was Oscar Olson.

The International Falls haul was eighty miles long, a greater distance, but straight. There the big hazards were a couple of narrow high grades with bridges where it was worth your life to try to meet anybody, but that was seldom a problem. It did happen one time, though, when glare ice prevented either of the drivers stopping as they approached the bridge from opposite directions, and one of them had to sluice his load to keep from slamming into the other. It was a suicide decision, but a miracle happened, and he's still alive to tell the tale.

The haul to the Grand Rapids mill was shorter, but there were plenty of narrow escapes for the truckers to hash over at the old West Hotel, between runs. My brother Norman was one near-victim. The drivers had to unload their trucks alone, tripping the binder chains and letting their loads rocket down onto the ice. This meant driving out on the river ice with a loaded truck, going to wherever the mill wanted the logs placed. Norman's load was just cascading down, when he realized that his truck had broken through the ice and he was headed for a watery grave. He got his door open and made a mighty leap for safety—but the force of the ice as the truck sank to the depth of the door slammed it shut, catching his foot. His co-pilot, Bob Prather, ran to his aid, and with super-human strength wrenched his rubber boot apart, freeing him. But did they give up trucking? Not on your life.

One winter my brother Hubert and Hans Ronning had contracts to haul pulpwood from the Loughran camp near Effie to International Falls, for the munificent sum of $2.50 a cord. The only way to beat the game was by high production, keeping the trucks on the road constantly. So Hub and Hans, with my brother Sam and I as opposite drivers, built a four-man shack on skids, equipped with a little gas plate, an airtight stove, and bunks, and towed it out to the job. The four of us would load the trucks in about half an hour (about seven cords, I suppose, of fairly light black spruce) and two drivers would take off for the Falls, unload, and return, doing the complete trip in about six hours. On their return, these two would cook pancakes, ham and eggs, fried potatoes, and coffee (the menu never varied). The other two, who had been snoozing in the bunks meanwhile, would be getting up and dressed. Quickly after eating we'd repeat the process of loading, and the two men who had slept would take the trips, while the other pair had their turn in the bunks. Sweat, freeze, eat, and sleep. We paid no attention to the clock, gaining about three hours in twenty-four on our three trips, so that by the week's end we'd have made sometimes twenty-three or twenty-four trips. But even at that pace, it wasn't enough to cover the expenses of tires, gas, and general wear and tear.

In rough, hilly country, Dave Patrow used a truck to pull a sleigh-load of logs. It worked well, and Dave kept up to the sawmill neck-and-neck. On one fateful trip, he felt the sleigh suddenly begin to sway, coming down the hill. He was not the only one to feel it—his passenger, old Jack Molan, became rigid and stared fixedly through the windshield, growling, "What's happening back there?" He figured they were about to get sluiced.

"Oh, she's swaying a little," Dave admitted cautiously, trying to control the fishtailing. Suddenly the sleigh slewed, struck a rock ledge close to the road, and splintered a runner.

They didn't have time to thank their stars that neither of them was hurt. Dave's first concern was the hauling: having no sleigh, how would they keep up to the mill? My father, Ivar Rajala, the camp blacksmith, was just as worried as he was. Both men knew they couldn't miss a trip or the operation would be shut down, and it was already evening. There was no way to get or make a four-inch heavy sleigh runner in the short time they had.

Then they remembered a sleigh belonging to one neighbor, on loan to another. "We'll get that runner," Ivar said. Together in the dark he and Dave went to the sleigh, which was parked in the farmer's yard, loaded with hay. They jacked it up, removed the runner, and took it back to their crippled vehicle, making the repair. To Dave's amazement they did all this without asking the farmer, or even telling him they were there. "No time now," Ivar said. "Can't lose the trip. We'll come back and pay him in the morning, or make him a new runner, whatever he wants. But now we got to get this sleigh running so's to keep up to the mill." Nonstop production was the name of the game.

The truck drivers of the exciting early days are the sensible, conservative older men of these times. Ned Patrow, Ole Torbenson, Erven Rahier, Bud Coolen, Pooch Liesenfeld, Earl Peloquin, Leslie Opsahl— every one of them has wild and funny stories to tell about freak accidents and ridiculous upsets, living in shacks so cold their hair froze to the pillow, missing death by a hair. But perhaps it's better not to tell them now. It wouldn't do for their kids to find out about the chances Granddaddy took in the days when earning a living was the main thing, and OSHA hadn't been heard from.

ONE-MAN CROSSCUT SAW

TEETH: 4 CUTTERS AND 1 RAKER

7

The Pain and Glory Boys

Paul had some funny experiences, driving logs. One time he drove on the Unreasonable River, that would run along a mile wide and two feet deep for a ways, and then it would turn on its side and be two feet wide and a mile deep. Another time, his men drove on the Round River, that ran in a circle, so that they finished up the drive right where they started.

Nothing in all the annals of logging has the excitement, the glamour, or the fascination of the log drive. Most people think of it as a time of high adventure, thrilling daredeviltry and hazardous activity. It was all that. Besides, it was slogging, backbreaking work, and required dogged endurance in the most miserable conditions of cold, wet, and hunger. Murderers in our prisons would riot for much less discomfort than one hour's work on the drive, but the "river pig" took it all in his stride and was proud to be part of it.

Almost anybody could be a river pig, but the "whitewater man" was special. He had to have skill, and courage, and determination. His balance on a rolling, plunging surface at the mercy of unseen obstructions and fickle current was a thing to marvel at. He lived with danger every minute, knowing that any misstep might be his last, and his mates would nail his boots to a tree and go on without him. They might be saddened, but the drive must go on, "come hell or high water."

With the coming of spring, the buildup of anticipation in the hamlets along the river would begin. Nothing compared with the excitement of watching the drive pass. Families living near Little Falls had a front-row seat on the banks. Others might not have such a vantage point, but the cry, "The drive's in!" brought school boys and adults down to the river side to watch the acrobatics of the river men (who occasionally put on a show of birling—spinning a log in the water by running on it, without falling off—for the entertainment of the bystanders, especially if some were pretty girls) and to sample the doughnuts and other goodies the cook prepared in quantities that never seemed depleted by these impromptu handouts.

Preparations for the drive had been made all winter. The logger piled his timber in rollways on the banks and on the ice of the rivers nearest his job. Logging was basically winter work, with the snow providing the hauling surface. When spring came, the grip of the ice would loosen. Melting snow and rain would swell the streams. Then came the thrilling, high-tension days of the Drive. The rollways would be "broken out," and the floods would carry the winter's cut downstream to the sawmill, or to the hoist where the logs would be loaded on railroad cars and taken to mills not on the watercourses.

The first chance for accident was right at the rollway, the high pile of logs parallel to the river that had to be jarred loose so the timber would cascade over the bank and into the water with a mighty splash. These were danger spots when piled high—they might roll out in any direction to crush or injure a man below "breaking the rollway."

The superintendent or his drive boss "walked the river"—followed its twisting course to search out hazards, dynamite out rocks, and in general second-guess the wily stream, noting the trouble spots. The drive boss received a consignment of peaveys and pike poles, made arrangements for the wanigan (the floating cook house), enlisted his crew, and the fever began.

A log drive was difficult. Death stalked the river banks. But the river men were equipped to deal with it in matter-of-fact terms. Their primary equipment was a pair of laced boots with caulks (called "corks")—sharp spikes in the soles and heels—a pike pole, long and slender with a sharp metal point on the end, and a peavey, a long metal point attached to a sturdy handle with a hinged hook for rolling logs. Running nimbly over the heaving, groaning mass of floating timber, they poked and shoved and pried, with peavey or pike pole, keeping the logs in motion, forcing them into the channel and preventing them from being caught on obstructions.

It's a rare man now who can boast of having worked on or witnessed a log drive on the Big Fork or Littlefork. Even at the time of the big drives, it was the high point of the year, and considered a treat not excelled by the fourth of July for drama and excitement.

There were drives along the Bigfork a good twenty years before the present century, as the canthook loggers, the timber pirates, and the earliest loggers moved their timber out of the area. Young men coming to live in the Big Fork Valley who worked in the camps during winter would sign on for the drive in spring, provided, of course, they had the spark of adventure and the sure-footed skills needed. You weren't asked if you could swim, but perhaps that may have dissuaded some of the more cautious homesteaders.

Boys today want to be hockey stars or astronauts, but the youth of the early 1900s dreamed of being "whitewater men," the sure-footed acrobats who rode the logs over the wild rapids and chutes of swift water.

Both Orin Patrow and Fred Peloquin were whitewater men. They both started out as very young men, and grew up with the log drives. Orin had already had his baptism in Wisconsin, along the Flambeau and Chippewa Rivers. When he "hove upon the scene" (as he expressed it) in the Big Fork Valley, he was experienced on the wild rivers.

Fred's first trip the full length of the Big Fork was as a cookee, in his early teens. This was an ideal experience. The wanigan drifted about five or six miles a day, average, and was moved between meals. At such times the young cookee sat in the bow watching the river as he peeled potatoes. He was greatly moved by the beauty of the river, with the swirling water and the banks richly overhung with giant green trees. Another pleasure was in cruising the woods with the wanigan man at every stop, for firewood, for there were no dry trees along the river; when one was found, they cut the whole tree and took it along. The thrill of going over the rapids in the wanigan, and the experience of portaging around Little Falls and Big Falls were overtopped by coming into the beautiful broad Rainy. On the American side all was wilderness, but there were some settlers in Canada. Along the banks, at Manitou Rapids and Sioux Rapids, Indians were drying sturgeon in the sun—though he noted that it was hard to see the sun for the flies around the fish. International Falls, known then as Koochiching, was a hamlet of only a few tarpaper shacks, most of which were unlicensed liquor sellers.

The logs, then, as they were for some years, were destined for mills at Rat Portage on Lake of the Woods, and were "boomed" and pulled across the lake by steamboats. For this purpose, always included in the drive were 150 boom sticks for each million board feet, cut near the river if possible. These were forty feet long, with butts and top ends hewed to twelve inches, and a three-inch hole bored twelve inches from each end. This fitted them for the chains that strung the booms together, making up the rafts for towing the logs.

The drive ended at Lake of the Woods, with an arduous trip back. A man could, of course, row a boat all the way up river. The more usual route was to take the steamboat Kenora to Fort Frances, the railroad from there to Port Arthur, the lake boat to Duluth, the Great Northern railroad to Deer River, and wait for the Minneapolis and Rainy River's next train day for a ride to Jessie Junction. From there, he walked to Turtle Lake, crossed in a rowboat, walked to Bello Lake, crossed in a boat again, and walked the final miles to Bigfork.

Having seen the glamour and excitement from such a vantage point, it is not to be wondered at that Fred worked on drives for many years following, becoming, along with Orin, one of the most sought-after foremen of his time.

The fortunes of the drive depended upon many variables—the weather particularly. A freshet of high water might spread the logs widely over meadows, and, receding suddenly, would leave the logs stranded on muddy banks and shallow bayous. High water was needed, but too high water might obscure the channel, and create invisible obstacles of unseen rocks or sweepers. The boss sweated through many nerve-wracking nights, wondering if his logs might lose their head of water through a sudden dry spell, and hang up his drive. Wind on a lake might stall the movement completely. Timing was critical, and tempers were short.

Orin Patrow was scheduled to bring down a big pine drive one year, when he learned to his consternation that Fred Peloquin would be in the river ahead of him with a cedar pole drive. This was considered something of a special hazard. If the water was running low, the long poles would jam in the rock rapids and become so entangled it was tough to break them loose. Fred was rated an expert jam breaker—Bill Byers remembers a drive he was on being held up by a monumental jam, at Wirt, and Fred being summoned to the scene from forty miles away, to break it—but anything could happen. Orin's heavy pine logs, following close, might compound the problem.

Orin was more than a little concerned when he spoke to Fred. "You get that cedar drive through, Peloquin, or there'll be hell to pay. If you get 'er hung in the rapids and I run a jam of pine on top of you, we'll never break 'er loose. I'll run right over you and smash your poles to toothpicks."

Fred was worried about the same thing, but luck was with him. The water was high from the snow melt, and spring rains. His drive ran full speed freely to the end at Rainy River.

On his way upstream, he met Patrow. The water was dropping fast. "By the Laird Harry, I'm glad to see ya," Orin said. "I may not get this pine through Big Falls, and I hate to leave this drive hung." So, tired though they were, Fred and his drivers turned to and helped put the pine drive through—just what Orin would have done if the shoe were on the other foot. Events like this cemented their friendship that continued as long as they lived.

Low water was not the only holdup. After a logging job for Namakan north of Camp 1, Orin was taking down the drive that consisted of his logs and those of Louie Pinette, Norway and jack pine. Coming down Deer Creek, he saw that the logs were jamming at Jack Young's meadows. An investigation showed that elm trees had been chopped into the creek, holding them back. On the bank sat Mrs. Young with a rifle, promising to shoot any driver who tried to put the drive through unless a toll was paid.

The drivers might have disputed the right of way with a man, but against a woman, they were helpless. Orin referred the matter to Archie Shaw, the walking boss of Namakan. No doubt the law would have upheld the loggers—blocking a waterway must have been illegal—but time was crucial. Namakan paid.

Nobody in the Big Fork Valley had the problem George Day did, just over the divide. He spent the winter landing his 300,000 feet of logs on a small lake, still known as Day Lake. When the ice melted, he waited for the spring torrents to whisk his logs out. It never happened: the lake had no outlet. His logs may be there yet.

A necessary adjunct to the log drive was the wanigan. As has been said, this was built like a houseboat, of planking caulked with oakum and tar. When it was moved through a rapids, four men with poles assisted, while the steersman had a big oar in the center of the stern.

The wanigan was built for one drive only, since bringing the unwieldly craft back upstream was never feasible. Consequently it could be tailored for the needs of that particular crew: a large wanigan for a big drive, a small wanigan for a small one. Some drives provided a bunk wanigan, some more than one, some allowed a minimum sleeping space on the cook wanigan. Many drives had only tents and blankets; often the men slept along the river bank in their wet clothes, on beds of balsam boughs.

On a wanigan they built for one of Patrow's drives, Fred and Prisque Peloquin painted a name: *Katharine Costello*, in honor of the school-ma'am Orin was courting, who subsequently became Mrs. Patrow. Usually, however, the clumsy scow was not considered worthy of such a distinction.

The wanigan was needed all the way, so it had to be got through rapids and falls. Around Big Falls, a team of drivers portaged it on rollers made of logs. Generally it was considered safe, if a bit hair-raising, to run it through rapids such as Little Falls.

A. D. Moors relates that when he went on drives, it seemed that he was always assigned to this activity. This would have been all well and good, but the other men on the detail (usually Ellis McLaughlin, Joe Danielson, Bob Pederson and Vic Lofgren) were tall, strapping men, while he was a head shorter and weighed only 125 pounds even when soaked. He was forced to put out extra effort on his quarter to hold his own. The bonus came after the wanigan got through—the grateful cook gave them a special meal.

If a low bridge loomed ahead, they usually detached the wanigan's roof to prevent damage. Going through the Deer Creek Rapids bridge when they hadn't observed this precaution, A. D. on the back of the wanigan was nearly wiped out when the bridge tore the roof off.

The wanigan cook had an endless job. He had to be up by three a.m., ready to feed the drivers at four. They ate again at nine or ten a.m., at two p.m., and finally supper was served at the end of the day, eight p.m. or dark. The lunch and "second breakfast" were sometimes brought to the men by the cookees. In between times, there were mountains of doughnuts, cakes, pies and bread to be prepared, much of which found its way into the stomachs of interested visitors who took it for granted that the hospitality of the lumber camp was continued on the drive.

Food was simple and sustaining. For breakfast the men ate pancakes, eggs, bacon, ham, and fried potatoes—no cake or pie, though it was a staple at all the other meals. It was good food, well cooked, and plenty of it. If an army moved on its belly, so did a log drive.

Sometimes the shortages of the season forced a cook to improvise. Mike Guthrie (later Minnesota's first forest ranger) remembered the unusual contribution of Stuttering Frank Smith when he was wanigan cook. Supplies on this particular drive were not especially fancy, running heavily to beans, sowbelly, potatoes and moose meat. Eggs in the springtime were a scarce commodity, but Frank somehow topped off one meal with a luscious cake. Pleased with the men's praise, Smith asked,

"D-d-d-do you know h-how m-m-many eggs in the c-c-c-cake?"

They of course couldn't guess. Smith said, "Th-th-thirteen!"

This was phenomenal, so far in the wilderness. The men were suitably impressed. Smith continued:

"D-d-d-do you know what k-k-kind of eggs they were?"

Again, mystification.

Smith said, "F-f-fresh t-t-turtle eggs."

Moving the wanigan was not generally the cook's responsibility, but on a small drive with a light wanigan, such might be the case. Mansel

Saunders was once a cook with this problem, with instructions to keep up to the driving crew to feed the drivers. When dinner time came, and no Mansel, Drive Boss Bob Pederson went looking for him. He found Mansel poling the wanigan frantically upstream. Somehow when he had been working inside, it had swung around without him noticing, and now he was doing his best to catch up—but headed the wrong way.

Sometimes wanigan cooks, if dissatisfied with their employers, might resort to odd means of revenge. One disgruntled fellow Frank Werthner remembered as being mighty liberal with gifts to folks along the river. They were not merely being served the pastries that were expected, but he was tossing out forty-pound hams and bacons to bystanders as well.

The day's work for the drivers was dark to dark, meeting whatever emergencies might arise in the course of the day. For this, Len Knotts recalled being paid $2.50 a day, which in time rose to $5.00 a day. This could result in a healthy stake some years—driving from the Upper Big Fork to Baudette took him 110 days, one season. Frank Werthner, on a different drive, spent eighty-five days to cover eighty-five miles.

Fred Peloquin's journal offers some interesting comparisons. It records that the drive he took down in 1922 began May 1, and lasted until May 26, with Craig being reached on May 20. For his services he was paid $185, plus an additional $84.55 which he didn't get until the next year. The 1923 drive, which started April 13, wound up May 17. His paycheck for that one was $224.60.

The drive developed its own lingo, along with the rest of the woods operations. Frequently heard along the river were such phrases as "Give 'er snoose," "Give 'er tarpaper," or "Give 'er tightass and popcorn," all of which meant the same thing: put out a bit of extra effort to move a log, "heave ho."

The drive boss had two responsibilities—his men and his logs. The most dreaded calamity on the log drive was the log jam.

Drivers worked forcefully and nimbly to keep the logs moving, but once in a while a big log might go berserk, or an obstruction develop that defied their efforts. One log would get hung up on a rock or other jillpoke, and trouble would start. A following log would be held back by the first log, and presently the river was bank-full of logs, thrusting and banging against each other, not able to move until the "key" log was pried loose and started on its way.

In order to prevent log jams in the most treacherous rapids, some specialists went ahead of the drive, blasting out large rocks with dynamite. Then, with oncoming logs, the men picked the right logs to build "wings" on either side of the main channel, thus raising the logs to the sides until the main channel was like a great chute. The bigger, heavier logs were slower, and drivers worked frantically to keep them moving in deep water. They crashed and banged into others with a "boom!" sometimes smashing into the wings and lodging there. Sometimes this would cause a new jam to start building, and the foreman would order half a dozen men to break a section of wing logs loose into the current.

When the water was low, the threat of a jam was constant. A huge jam of Namakan logs—fifty million feet—built up at Little Falls, reaching ten feet above the rocks and water. Logs backed up upstream for four miles. Elmer Knotts, charged with keeping the logs moving through Little Falls, used all his dynamite with no results; still the backup continued. The Namakan superintendent, Dunc Price, was jumping up and down with worry and excitement, and finally became so ill from the stress he had to lie down on the river bank. Knotts' helper, Roy Wakeman, saw what had to be done.

"If you'll go down there with me, we'll turn the logs that are stuck and get this thing going," he told Knotts. They did—and she "hauled"! When the jam burst, the men ran for their lives over a hundred yards across the bobbing logs, reaching shore in time to see the plugged river gush loose, flinging logs over the banks as the torrent rushed by full width. It broke trees that were eighteen inches in diameter, sweeping them down like dominoes, and small logs were reduced to splinters from the weight of the thousands of tons of onrushing logs through the narrow channel. But it hauled clean through the "sny."

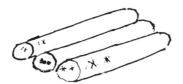

STAMPS AND BARK MARKS ON LOGS
IX, B&B, ꓘK

There were other big jams. One, at Muldoon Rapids, held up a drive for fifteen days in a four-mile conglomeration of tangled logs, bank-full and wedged tight, backed up to Busti's landing. They were mixed logs, from several companies, with cedar poles and post mixed in. Frank Werthner along with twenty other men spent weeks "dry-picking" (dragging the logs to the channel without water), until, with the pressure released, it broke loose. With a thunderous racket of groaning and crashing that could be heard for miles, it hauled clean, with the small cedars ground up into slivers and the force of the torrent washing the whole drive clear to Big Falls, seventy miles away.

A late start, and problems with the booms, seemed to jinx a drive of Backus' logs one year. It was a huge gathering of big pine logs from several hundred-man camps. But the booms on Deer Lake mysteriously broke, scattering the big pine all over the lake. A man named Cameron was hired to round them up, at fifty cents per thousand—a tidy sum, when applied to two million feet. The men spent weary time rounding them up. They had scarcely finished when a terrific wind arose, and again the booms broke. The gathering seemed to take forever, booming up the scattered logs, winching them up by manpower on small raft "headworks." These were manned by eight men on each raft to turn the sweep arms and capstan, winding up the booms. Logs were gathered together, tied in a bunch called a "brail," with a ring on a pointed iron pounded into the end, and wire holding, until they got enough for a boom. With no current, it was push, push, push. Frank Werthner and Mike Guthrie thought the job would never be finished.

Suspicious that there was some skullduggery behind their unexplained misfortune, the company hired an armed guard. Right or not, it seemed to cure the problem.

Jack Young's wife wasn't the first to hit upon the idea of a toll extracted from logging companies. A Battle Lake logger of the 1880's had worked for the Rat Portage Company, and gave his name to a farm camp known as "Stitt's ranch." His brainstorm was to charge the company forty cents per thousand for sluicing their logs down Upper Dam of Deer Creek. The company protested, and built Lower Dam further down stream, making his dam useless. But Stitt wasn't through—he had filed a stone and timber claim along the creek, which effectively prevented the company from flooding his land. They gave up, and paid the toll.

A jam of a different sort beset Vic Lofgren's crew in 1914 on a drive for Engler, at Craig. They weren't unprepared for it. The log booms for Backus and Brooks' hoist took up more than half the river, and impeded the movement of logs. The walking boss, Ross Slack, gave Vic his instructions, secretly, along with an extra supply of dynamite. The hoist would have to be destroyed.

It was, however, easier said than done. Knowing the problem their hoist created, Backus and Brooks had all-night guards to prevent any sabotage to the thirty-eight piling that held the boom.

The drive reached Craig; the logs in the river slowed, stopped, and built up in a three-mile jam. Vic, meanwhile, spent two days visiting Craig and reconnoitering (and enjoying the hospitality and firewater of the place). He could see no time when the hoist was unguarded at night, and during the day, the hoisting crew was about. He soon realized that the hoist could not be blown at night. It would have to be a daylight job.

Next day, thirty-eight picked men with thirty-eight long poles, pointed on one end and soaped, with twenty sticks of dynamite lashed to each pole, moved stealthily under the cover of the bank to the crucial spot. They stopped at the appointed spot and waited, hushed, for the signal: the noon whistle. When it blew, none of the hoisting crew would be looking anywhere but at their lunch. At the sound of the whistle, each man planted his stick, loaded with explosives, on the piling that was his assigned objective. Within seconds, all the area rocked with a tremendous CRASH! as 760 sticks of dynamite blew at once. Craig's denizens got an unholy awakening that morning. Eyewitness said saw-logs filled the air for half an hour. The jam stirred and heaved slightly, like a kettle of oatmeal on the boil, then boiled over, uprooting trees, and carrying hoist and boom timbers before it down the foaming current. As for the hoist, it was never rebuilt. Backus took the equipment to International Falls.

Years of log driving gave Frank Werthner experiences of all kinds, in weather that was sometimes merely miserable, and often downright wretched. It snowed hard on the Muldoon one May 14, and with four inches of the white stuff built up on the logs, the men could hardly keep their footing. When a man slipped into the water between logs, the boss gave orders to knock off. Their wet, cold tents gave no comfort, but Bob Pederson and some others found an old root cellar. After they'd warmed it with a hot fire, they let the fire die down and entered. They spent a couple of days in comfort in this windowless dugout.

Unless the bullcook was careful where he pitched your tent, in wet weather, it was no guarantee of refreshing rest. In a hard rain, below Little Falls, a streamlet of water coursed right through Frank's tent and those of others as well. Grumbling, the men slogged through the storm to an old barn near by—all except Frank, who was so tired he slept in spite of being drenched. They awoke to a new misfortune: a homesteader, always on the lookout for lumber, had seen their unprotected jargos and helped himself. They had to scrounge the river bank for boards to make repairs.

One memorable season, he started from Wirt while it was still bitterly cold, with floating ice. Wanigans were ready, and the water high, with logs spread out on the big flats. But a sudden drop in temperatures had frozen an inch of ice, and caused Frank's legs and feet to become cramped and lame. Vic Lofgren was concerned, and urged him to go as cookee instead of driver, but there would be no waiting; the drive would start. Frank's pride would not let him accept this coddling. He decided to tough 'er out.

The men had to jump on the frozen logs to break them loose from the ice, and sent them down river, stopping from time to time to warm themselves at the bank fires. After a few hours of this, Frank discovered that his rheumatic pains had disappeared. They never bothered him again. Perhaps doctors have overlooked a simple cure for arthritis. Certainly, I can't recall a single old river driver who was crippled with it.

Frustration mounted as they continued to have cold weather. When they reached Big Falls, where a jam had built up due to low water, an icy rain was beginning. Men in gangs of four to six worked in the sleet, dragging logs over the falls, wet through—(a man wearing a raincoat on the drive would have been hooted out of the country). Frank thought he was drowning standing up. He threw down his peavey, saying, "I won't work in this for anybody!" and started up the bank.

He found himself face-to-face with Vic Lofgren, who growled, "Who the hell told you to?"

Frank was sure he was fired, and kept on his way. Turning at the top, he saw the whole crew following, with Lofgren bringing up the rear.

The men bedded down on the wanigans, which had been portaged around the falls, and slept as exhausted men will, while the downpour continued. At daybreak they woke to an earth-shaking rumble as logs came thundering and cracking. At the falls was a staggering sight. Small logs, big logs, tumbled and crashed over the falls as the jam hauled, grinding up smaller timber, with the thirty-foot and forty-foot boom sticks chained together whirling end-over-end, piling and all, as the Duluth Logging Company's sawmill sorting hoist and bull chain was swept away. The deluge had saved them from the grind of dry-picking, but instead left them with the job of salvaging the chains and untangling them from the boom sticks. This could only be done by the dangerous work of sawing and chopping out on the rocks.

Booms might be used for other purposes than sorting and rafting. In the flat country along Deer Creek, walking booms were built to keep logs in the channel.

Big logs, floating low in the water and ready to hang up at any obstacle, caused most problems. Cork pine, such as the Titanic camp drove one year, bobbled along with two-thirds of the log above water.

Dams with gates controlled the water level. The familiar dams on Deer Creek, built to eliminate swift rocky rapids, were made by laying down chute logs or timbers, split as slabs from large White Pines, a foot thick and twenty-four feet long. These were anchored into the ledge-rock on long cross beams dug into both banks, and fastened with long iron drift pins, the top ones overlapping the lower set by four inches, and side walls constructed. The operative part was the gate, which could be opened when a good head of water was impounded, sluicing the logs over the rapids that lay below the nine-foot waterfall.

The opening of the dam was a scheduled operation, usually at one-hour intervals. Logs were worked into the center of the stream, a warning was shouted to the men below, and the gate was opened, washing the logs down with the flood. By building up a head of water overnight, they could sluice logs down all day.

Building a dam on Coon Creek, in a rock ledge, gave special problems because of the crack in the rock that wasn't plugged even by re-inforcement with concrete. The dam in, the channel had to be opened, and the men had dynamite in fifty-pound boxes for the purpose. A big hollow tamarack stump close to the dam resisted their efforts, and Frank Magnusson, the dynamite man, tried a special method. He put the explosive into the stump, and topped it with a round rock. The crew took to the woods for safety and watched developments.

The blast went off with satisfactory effect, and they drifted back. They were met by their cook, wild-eyed, his hair on end, liberally bespat-tered with beans. There were beans in his hair, all over his face and clothes, and down his neck, and he was loudly perturbed more than somewhat. The rock had fallen through the cook-camp roof, smashing the beanpot and the stove, and throwing beans all over the place.

Much earlier, a pre-1900 camp had cut a new channel at Battle Lake, allowing logs to shortcut across a peninsula into Pickerel Lake. There was also early evidence of changes in the channel of Deer Creek, elimi-nating its meander into Pinette (Mudhen) Lake, and an old low dam where Deer Creek leaves Deer Lake. This was international water, but no one seems to have bothered to get a permit.

To cross Deer Lake and Pickerel Lake, much booming and rafting was done. Most of this involved rafts, with "headworks;" good-sized logs spiked together, with a capstan mounted in the middle with two or four sweep arms. Four men manned each arm (unless horsepower was used) turning the capstan spool, and a man coiled the rope. It was tedious work, winching and towing the logs against westerly head winds, but it did the job.

When the boom of logs was winched to the headworks on the raft, the three-hundred-pound anchor was weighed, carried forward in a bateau to the length of the tow rope, and dropped. Then they winched the raft up to it for a new "bite." The whole process was repeated until the boom of logs was moved across the lake.

Charley Bibeau worked on a big side-wheeler tug where the crew of three handled the forty-foot rope: one coiling, one pulling slack, and one standing by. Horses, of course, hauled bigger booms on larger rafts.

Charles Bibeau worked mostly on a bateau, bringing up the rear. This meant rounding up the logs that had lodged against the banks or in other ways escaped their destiny. These craft were also called sacking boats. One year, wild rice so hampered log movement late in the season, the sacking crew had to cut it with scythes to get their charges moving.

Normal pay was three dollars a day, but Bibeau's special expertise earned him a secret deal of fifty cents extra. Others of the crew, discontented with the slogging grind, threatened to strike, unless their pay was raised. A crippling strike in the middle of a drive could spell disaster, but the head office met their demand head-on: they told foreman Bob Pederson to fire the whole crew, and hire a new one.

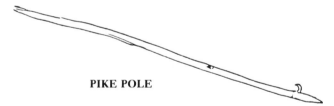

PIKE POLE

Charles Bibeau never got his wish to follow the drive all the way to the Rainy, but A D Moors did—three times, in drives of eighty million feet or more, sometimes one hundred million. Indeed, in his belief the smallest drive was thirty-nine million feet for Backus. Many summers that he recalled, the pine logs ran in a steady stream from early spring until fall, with crews one after another chasing their logs down river to the mills.

He started at fifteen, for Engler, and went on to work until World War I. In time he knew all the celebrated names: the Knight brothers, Jim and Godfrey—"good men, and fast on logs, with Jim one of the best drivers ever on the river;" Joe Danielson, who could snap a peavey handle in his hands; Hungry Mike Sullivan; Haywire O'Connell; Dunc Price; Archie Shaw; Ross Slack; Happy Jim Rahier, who "could ride a cedar tie as if he was glued to it;" Fred Peloquin—"a real good man anywhere in the woods, and like a squirrel on logs, able to get a crew working together in the most crucial places, break a jam of the worst kind and make 'er haul," Bob Pederson, who had the cold-steel nerve for any chances, even though he couldn't swim; Vic Lofgren, who "wasn't scared of anything;" and Orin Patrow, the dean of them all.

Vic Lofgren recruited A D from Deer River one year, first to help get the wanigans ready. Then Vic said, "Could you walk to Bigfork tomorrow and get a crew?" It was a long, weary hike, from early morning until nearly dark, with still the task of rounding up a crew. The next morning saw them on the way to Wirt, another tiring march. One crew member (the wild and woolly Ellis McLaughlin) dropped from hangover-induced illness and fatigue, so that A D found himself hauling the ailing man's packsack ("about the size of a table") with a peavey and pikepole to boot. The two days' long hard effort began to tell on A D, but he pushed on. When he finally got to the wanigan all he could do was climb on it and sit, while the trees seemed to sway back and forth.

With Joe Danielson, he poled the rear, riding a log down one side of the river the five long miles to Harrison Hill, where the crew was putting in rollways. A D, a mere stripling, could easily find a log that would float with him on it, but for Joe, a hundred pounds heavier, it was a harder search.

Dunc Price was a familiar figure on the log drives. As walking boss (superintendent) of Namakan, known to be wealthy, he needn't have subjected himself to such rigors, but he seemed to think it was fun. When ever he thought it necessary, he'd jump right out of the bateau into the icy water, to help the crew roll the big pines back into the stream. "We gotta get these big ones," he would say.

Coming down in the boat with A D, he spotted a few big trees left by loggers growing along the river bank. He would insist on the men's taking a crosscut, sawing 'em down and rolling 'em in with the rest of the drive. Some grinning went on behind his back, at the idea of a millionaire wanting to work so hard for one more pine tree.

Archie Shaw was a man respected as much for his personality as his position as superintendent. Quiet, educated, and cultured, he nevertheless understood the drivers and their needs, and was aware of what had to be done. When a big jam developed at Rice River rapids, Shaw went ahead to the point where a man had been stationed, to keep the drive moving, and found the man asleep in the sunshine. He said mildly, "Ace, you'd better wake up—you're going to get sunburned."

Not that it was fun and games, by a long shot. More than one driver, working above Big Falls, slipped and fell, with rescue attempts failing. Bob Pederson (every boy's idol as the boss with dash and daring), breaking up a jam against a big rock, lost his footing and was about to be sucked under into the furious torrent when Vic Lofgren shoved out his pike pole and hauled him to safety. Vic himself had been saved in just the same place and manner years earlier by Fred Peloquin, plucked from a log he was riding that was about to go over the falls. Ralph Rosing fell from a tipping jargo while working to break a wild center, and was drowned at Dell Rapids. And there were others who fell but didn't live to tell about it.

The family most marked by tragedy in the Big Fork Valley was the Harringtons, handsome lively men. First was Dewey, who slipped into six feet of water from a log boom, while crossing Deer Creek as he was carrying lunch to the crew. The heavy pack trapped him on the bottom. His brother, Pete, returning across the boom in the evening, found him there.

Though the other family tragedies were unrelated to the drive, they gripped the imagination and sympathy of those who knew the family: Dean Harrington, a fireman on a locomotive hauling timber on Backus' railroad, was a victim when the engineer disobeyed orders with a heavier-than-proper train and made a race for the grade. The speeding engine topped the hill, jumped the track, crashed through a four-hundred-foot-long stack of pulp wood, and overturned. Dean, pinned underneath, was scalded to death. When a truck accident claimed Tom, a third son, the family was thereafter considered star-crossed.

Charles Bibeau rescued three men, at various times on the drive. One awkward greenhorn tipped his raft into a wing, was pitched off, and was pulled to safety by grabbing Bibeau's pike pole. A similar rescue happened when an awkward man's pike pole slipped, causing him to fall in; that time, Bibeau had to fish around with his own pike pole before finding the man, who was already blue, but did survive. The third rescue was a freak accident, when Jim Robinson jumped from a log to what he thought was a sand bar, around which logs were eddying. It was quicksand, and quick it slid, with Robinson immediately sinking. Bibeau gave him his pole to cling to, while working logs to within the man's reach for him to cling to for safety.

Frank Werthner was nearly a casualty when cleaning up the rear below Big Falls. With his partner Louis Caldwell (of the Caldwell Brook smallpox camp family), he was working behind the main crew, riding a jargo on one side of the river while two men on another jargo were clearing the other side. A jargo, a raft of four or five light, easy-running logs spiked together with planks, with wooden grocery boxes for seats when the men were merely riding and not on their feet poling logs, is not the most maneuverable craft. As the current carried them, they saw ahead, directly in their path, a big Balm-of-Gilead sweeper—a tree tipped into the river—with its stump and four or five feet under the high water, and the top stretching out into the river. Their twelve-foot pike poles wouldn't reach bottom. With no way to guide their course, they had no alternative but to see themselves being swept into the tree top, and brushed off their jargo, which would tip and go under the branches. And neither man could swim.

Their only chance was to maneuver the jargo broadside, grab the tree top, and try to regain the jargo with their pike poles when it surfaced just beyond the treetop. When it struck, they grabbed the branches as the overturned raft shot underneath—but Louis lost his pole. Frank reached as far as he could, but the jargo eluded him. There they were, marooned in midstream, the other jargo out of sight beyond a curve, and the main crew far forward. It was too deep to wade to shore. The prospect was gloomy.

Frank realized they had only one hope. The superintendent, Ross Slack, did patrol the river several times a day in his motor launch. If they could hold on, perhaps he might come in time.

But they did not have to wait for Slack. When the raft, bottom side up, and the floating lunches and grocery boxes caught up with the drive, downstream, Vic Lofgren went into action at once. With A D Moors, he hurried back upstream, wading waist-deep along the flooded banks, hollering. Frank and his partner answered.

Vic stopped at the tree. "Take off your coats, and throw them here," he ordered. Then he walked the tree trunk, wading until the water reached his shoulders. He told Frank to reach out with his pole as far as he could—but it barely reached Vic's grasp. "Hang on for all you're good for, and let go the tree," Vic said, and hauled Frank in like a beaver swimming in the water. The nervous Caldwell was rescued in the same manner, after which they all rejoined the drive. A few days later they were at it again in another jargo—but from then on, their pike poles in deep water were sixteen feet long.

As it happened, Ross Slack did come down, later that day. He said, "I wish I'd-a seen you guys—I'd-a waved and gone right by and left you." Not that he meant it. This was just another example of the teasing cry of other drivers when men fell, as happened several times a day: "Never mind the man—save the peavey!"

Humor was needed to lighten the grim facts of life. Much of it was directed at the inexperienced. One particular greenhorn was charged very soberly with the responsibility of measuring the water levels. He was instructed to mark a board at one inch intervals, nail it on the wanigan, and report daily how matters stood. He dutifully checked his board each day, but nothing seemed to change. Two days of heavy rain caused him to rush out, hoping to see how much the downpour registered. He didn't understand until he heard the guffaws of the crew.

Old hands enjoyed fooling greenhorns at the oxbow below Little Falls. Here the river makes a hairpin turn, coming back almost besides itself for some distance, only a hundred yards or so away. "Lookit there," they'd say pointing at the men poling frantically in an opposite direction. "Them guys are driving the logs back upriver."

Len and Dutch Knotts got their feet wet at an early age, helping their father keep Little Falls clear. Like Tom Gunderson, Len, who couldn't swim, claimed to have waded the full length of the Big Fork from Bowstring to the Rainy. Their biggest problems came with the sixteen-foot logs, which have a tendency to run crosswise at the head of the falls and wedge into a narrow gap after going over the nine-foot drop. Even increasing the crew couldn't keep the jam from crowding down. They finally licked the problem by fastening the logs to trees in the forest above the falls, until the blockage below was cleared. Then they chopped the cables, and the pressure from above hauled out the whole river clean as a whistle.

Good-natured men like Joe Danielson were an asset, and his strength was proverbial. He didn't need a helper. Rolling a big log with his peavey in his right hand, with his left hand he used Len's peavey, and with a mighty reef rolled the log free. Joe liked to ride the big logs known to the drivers as "homesteaders" from their propensity to stop off along the way, sitting with a pike pole across his knees, lunchbag handy, playing nonchalantly on his mouth organ. Frequently he was point man, going ahead to trouble spots. "Keep the logs moving" was the watchword, as none knew better than Joe.

An odd quirk of nature which drivers frequently observed was the habit logs had of eddying in a large whirlpool, in places at the foot of a waterfall or below a dam where washing waters had formed a large basin. During the day they would continue their endless cycles, circling, circling, but at night the pool would empty and next morning it would be clear. No one could give a reason, though many told of seeing it.

Where the Big Fork emptied into the Rainy, the drive ended. The boom company took the logs, sorting them for the mills. Each log bore an end stamp, made with the stamp hammer, which branded into the wood a mark that identified the company owning it and the sale from which it was cut. These marks were registered in the state surveyor general's office much as cattle brands were registered. Further identification was by means of the bark mark, axe-hewn into the log surface. Men recognized these at a glance with easy familiarity, and the sorting went rapidly, with a man stepping on the end of a half-submerged log to expose the identifying stamp, or giving it a whirl with his "corked" boots to show the bark mark.

The driving over, the men dispersed. Some went home to their farm work, some went to work in the harvest fields of North Dakota (it was often nearly that season, before the drive ended), some followed the tradition to "go down" and blow their stake.

Traditionally this often ended in epic battles, as the men who were the toughest on the river tested who was toughest on land.

It was also a way to let off steam, to pay back or punish slights that had to be ignored during the duration of the drive. Vic Lofgren once came to A D Moors, seething: "If I hit Ellis McLaughlin, will you back me up?" A D snorted. "Vic, are you crazy? Ellis McLaughlin'll lick both of us!" A D was still in his teens, but he had seen Ellis McLaughlin in action. "Vic was tough," he said, "but that Ellis was a powerful brute, fast as a buzz-saw."

An easy-going man who was a tiger when aroused was Joe Danielson. In a street fight with another bruiser he was on the ground, about to get a pair of boots applied to his head. It looked like he was a goner, but he crawled up out of there, got to his feet, and began kicking his opponent. When the man had had enough, Joe ordered him out of town.

Pete Apple, who came to the Valley from Michigan, well-scarred from battles in which someone "put the boots to 'im,'" had plenty of rough-and-tumble experience, and was always ready to raise Cain. The brotherhood of free-for-all fighters was not large, but there were enough members to provide excitement for those who craved it.

The big men often avoided fights, preferring to enjoy their drinks in peace,—if the quarrelsome ones would permit. Charles Bjornson, by all accounts capable of flattening all comers, was known to push trouble-makers against the wall, saying, "Now, damn you, behave yourself or I'll slap your face." But generally speaking, the tradition of tearing the town apart after a drive never quite caught on among the Big Fork Valley men.

All things considered, not many deaths occurred on the log drives on the Big Fork. On the other hand, a death occurred in a case when a man didn't go on the drive after finishing the winter's work. Instead, while drinking, he intruded at an Indian camp, forced a man out of his tepee, and spent the night with the woman. The Indian went for a weapon. Returning the next morning with a twenty-gauge shotgun, he blasted the man with buckshot. It wasn't immediately fatal, but it was a powerful deterrent. The other Indians at the encampment realized the seriousness of the act, and reported it to the log drivers who brought the victim to their camp. The man lingered for seventeen days but could not recover. His grave at the Deer Creek Farm Camp can still be found.

A man who was legendary among river drivers was Hungry Mike Sullivan, often a drive boss. He knew the job, and had young drivers at every bend of Deer Creek, crowding them hard to work. He thought himself a singer (though nobody who heard him agreed), and his bellering could be heard for miles.

He was not averse to doing a full man's work himself. On a mean, cold day, with big logs hung up in a channel, Frank Werthner was preparing unhappily to wade in and dislodge the logs when Hungry Mike came along.

"Never mind, me bye [boy], I'm all wet, anyway," he sang out. Into the water like a big bull moose he went, loosening the logs and sending them on their way.

Innocent lads were frequently taken in by Mike's guileless question, "Me bye, do ye have any tea?" Of course the young drivers offered the boss their lunch bucket, "hanging up there in the tree." Hungry Mike was said to have disposed of a dozen or so lunch baskets in this manner, some days. "Boil da pot" was the signal to hide part of their lunches.

He happened upon Joe Danielson tending dam on Deer Creek, with the same question. Joe offered the tea he had, about half a gallon in a five-gallon lard can. Mike drank that down, and asked Joe to make some more, with something to eat. Joe couldn't very well refuse the drive boss, so he pulled out his provisions—half a loaf of bread and some ham. Hungry Mike devoured it all, and polished off Joe's apple pie and some doughnuts. Then he spent the evening by Joe's fire, amiably telling him stories, and finally curled up to sleep, leaving Joe with nothing for supper.

Frank Werthner encountered him at a Deer Creek tent camp, from which the cook had decamped with the grub. He was detailed by Mike to catch fish with hooks and line Mike produced from somewhere, and he did: using salt pork for bait, he caught perch which he used to catch walleyes, thirteen of them, all two-or-three-pounders. The new cook fried them nicely and set them on a log to await the hungry crew.

Mike got there first. He wolfed down every one, leaving none for the men.

He did the same thing when the cook stewed the leg of a deer a crew member had shot. Men told of seeing him finish off a small roast pig and all the trimmings. His capacity became a matter of legend.

In the final chapter, Frank met Hungry Mike in Deer River years later. He was almost unrecognizable, thin and drawn, a ghost of his former self, having just been released from the hospital after surgery for "stomach trouble." The cause of his immense hunger was revealed—in an operation, surgeons removed a thirty-three-foot tapeworm.

My father was on log drives, though not every year. Sometimes his farm work needed him. Perhaps he lost interest because of early experiences.

In one of his first drives, near Muldoon rapids, a tornado swept through, picking up logs and water, carrying them up the hillside and strewing them all about, leaving the river bed empty. The men were terror-stricken and ran for safety, all the while being deluged by flying logs, rocks, mud, and sheets of water. The wild confusion was over in minutes, but the extent of the damage was colossal.

DRIVER'S BOOTS & PIKE POLE ON LOG

The dazed men were faced with the miserable task of dragging, rolling, and rossing the wayward logs back into the river. Six or eight men with peaveys can move an amazingly heavy log, weighing three thousand pounds or more, and they all gave their best efforts. But the disheartening clean-up job took many weary days.

The big wind did other damage, elsewhere—it broke boom chains, scattered logs all over Deer Lake, and drove them back upstream. Rounding them up took several weeks, using the man-powered winches on rafts and the system with the three-hundred-pound anchor. It was disspiriting work, not at all the sort my father liked best, and gave little sense of accomplishment.

Sluicing logs down Deer Creek with a crew, Father was right in the thick of it. But one rush of water came without the customarily-shouted warning. The flood washed over him and the logs he was working, washing man and logs out of the creek and into the Big Fork River a mile downstream.

One spring he was sent down to Deer Creek to get a huge cork pine lunker, six feet in diameter, that hadn't made it down the drive in several years. With the high water, he finally got it down, and eventually Vic Lofgren and Bob Pederson steered it into Jim Reid's mill. But it was a doubtful victory—it broke the log hoist, going up, and it took most of a day to get it through the mill. Big though it was, it cost many times the worth of its sawed lumber, and Reid would have been better off if he'd left it in the river where it lay.

My brother Art went on drives, starting when he was sixteen. Green new young men were usually initiated by being put in the rear crew, which meant jumping into the icy waters to pick up stragglers. It was cold and miserable, snowing while they were breaking rollways, but there was no turning back. Bob Pederson and Vic Lofgren, the bosses, assured my father that they would give Art a fair shake, and watch that he took no foolish chances.

Not everyone was that helpful. One cranky fellow working logs around a sweeper, with Art on the outboard end of the same log, took advantage of the opportunity to give the log a sudden twist with his corks, expecting to pitch the younger driver into the deep, cold water. Art caught his balance just in time, but in doing so he threw his partner off balance, and *he* took the dive in the drink. When the older man begged for mercy, Art pulled him out.

His stint as a driver was short-lived. One morning at daylight, Bob Pederson came to him with new orders: "Get to the cook wanigan, and start breakfast right now. The cook's gone off on a drunk and taken the hams and bacons to pay for his toot, and we've got to feed the men."

Art protested that he was not a cook, but Pederson was the boss. "Feed 'em pancakes and potatoes," he said, and took off on the run to hire a new cook. His not to reason why, Art removed the empty whiskey bottles and did the best he could.

Reaching Big Falls, they had the not-unusual jam, with logs piled as high as the bridge. The immediate danger was that the bridge would go out, but the dynamite man was gone, presumably on a spree. Bob's younger brother Paddy was prepared to do the job, but it was tricky business for one man alone. Art volunteered to go along.

Bob said, "You're too young."

But the younger men insisted, and there was no time to lose in debating. Bob okayed the project, but warned them to cut long fuses, light them at the same time, and hang on to the ropes for dear life when the crew pulled them up. There were no slip-ups: the charges went off, blowing logs sky-high; the jams roared down through the falls in an awesome spectacle, and the men watched in a glow of satisfaction. They'd saved the bridge.

The glamour and excitement of the log drive were the only facets of it that impressed me as a boy. We knew that in the spring the grand spectacle would come, and we prepared for it. Several of us neighborhood boys would cut firewood in the winter, haul it down to the river bank on bob sleds, and pile it, against the time of the spring thaw.

At that time, every afternoon after school, we boys would run the mile to the river, hoping to see the log drive come. The big boys carried this one step farther, helping to push the logs through, though the drivers or bosses often chased them away when they caught them, telling them it was "too dangerous for kids."

When the wanigan arrived, and tied up at the foot of Deer Creek rapids, our time had come. We would offer our firewood to the cook or bullcook, bartering it for the goodies they had to offer, with the smell of frying doughnuts in our nostrils making our mouths water. It didn't matter that the smell of tar and pitch was equally strong. All the more wonderful to us.

It was a real day for us when the cook paid us off in grub, and invited us aboard the wanigan. He'd hand us tin plates and cups, and tell us to "fill up" on ham, potatoes, coffee or tea, then fill up again on pie and other goodies. On leaving, the cook might give us a pie, or a sack of doughnuts and cookies. Some lucky years we even collected a few dollars in change besides, but whatever the deal, everybody was happy.

We would watch for hours the drama of the men on the river. I remember seeing Big Bob Pederson, the foreman, and his gang riding down on a broken wing section, with the logs tossing and rolling everywhich-way when it began to break up. I watched him steering a big log for the nearest solid wing, shouting above the crashing and banging of the mad melee of men and logs, "Jump for shore!" Nearly all made it, but one fell short, scrambling up on the wing logs just in the nick of time ahead of the rush of logs into the boiling rapids. He was minus his hat and peavey, and they all laughed, ridiculing him. To them it was just another incident in the day's work.

We held our breath at the thrill when the five-man crew steered the big wanigans through the swift current of the rapids at terrific speed, with Big Bob shouting, "Hold 'er to the left!" as they flew straight down the chute, miraculously missing the rocks. Then they went back for the roof, which had been removed because high water would have prevented its passing safely under the bridge, and brought it down and replaced it after the wanigan had tied up below.

The last drive to the northern mills came down the Littlefork in 1937, after the deepest-snow winter men could ever remember. The eight feet of snow in the woods turned to water all at once when the spring thaw came, and the thirteen million feet of pine logs, piling, cedar poles, ties, and 30,000 cords of pulpwood piled into the river and went a-sailing.

I had worked in the woods that winter myself, with snow so deep that in heavy timber we who were skidding had to work the same trails day after day, or they would become so clogged with snow the horses could not travel them. You could barely see the top of the horses' heads from one skidding trail to the next, as each was like a trough.

We knew that this drive faced unexpected hazards, and wondered how matters would go.

We soon found out. Bulldog Hanson called one night for my father to gather all cables, clamps, chains, and tackle that he had, and send it by truck with Norman to Camp 29, to pick up all they had there, and drive with all possible speed to the Littlefork River bridge. High waters were threatening a big jam that would tear out the bridge, and all available equipment was needed to secure it by anchoring it to trees and stumps. Delivering the tackle, we were told by the bridge crew that from the force of the logs and water the bridge did move a foot, but serious damage was averted.

(In the fall of 1979, this old bridge was torn down and a new one built to replace it. It was observed that the old bridge had been swayed considerably out of alignment by the force of water and the big log jam.)

The drive reached its destination, in accordance with the fatalistic slogan of the old drivers, "Come hell or high water." They had both. It was a sight that was never repeated, and I'm sure never will be. The action was photographed by a genuine whitewater man, Carl Hendrikson, one of two lumberjacks of whom I know that wore Phi Beta Kappa keys, and the only one with the distinction of having lost his in the waters of the Littlefork. It's fitting and fortunate that moving pictures of the event survive, showing to those who will never see it some of the thrill and hardship that made it the climax of the logging season. To those of us who remember something of the way it was, it brings a sadness and regret for those daring young devil-may-care men, the like of whom will never be seen again.

PEAVEY

8

Daylight in the Swamps

Sourdough Sam was Paul's cook. His pancake griddle was so big he couldn't get it greased, until he thought of tying bacon rinds to the cookees' feet and letting them skate over the surface. The bookkeeper was Johnny Inkslinger, always trying to make things more efficient. One summer he saved several barrels of ink by not crossing his t's and dotting his i's. He ran a hose from the barrel of ink to his pen, and that was the first fountain pen.

The blacksmith was Big Ole. He made Babe's shoes, and they were so heavy he sank into the ground a foot at every step, when he was carrying them to the barn. Shot Gunderson was camp foreman. One year he landed the logs on a lake that didn't have an outlet, but he knew what to do. He just emptied the icing-tank wagon into the lake and raised the level so the logs floated overland to the mill. It was the same when Chris Crosshaul, the straw boss, sent the wrong logs down the river. Babe just drank out of the river and sucked the water backwards, and floated 'em right back.

The jack's home away from home was the camp. Just as a "house" is not a home, so also the manner of construction, the materials and style, and the presence or absence of certain niceties which helped characterize the camp were not the factors that decided whether or not it was a "good" camp.

Jacks didn't expect luxurious accommodations. Ordinarily a camp was planned for one season's occupancy, though in some cases it could be used for many years. There wasn't much point in making fancy housing for six-months' use.

In early times there were camps built from first-class pine logs, the biggest available—and therefore the fewest needed—for one winter's use. When the job was over, sometimes the buildings were dismantled and the timbers hauled to the river, to float in the spring log drive.

A camp frequently had a history. Men such as Dan McLeod, who had been on the scene as a scaler for Rat Portage and Keewatin Companies, had recollections of camps at certain locations. Many people could pinpoint the Horseshoe camp (named at a time when oxen were the chief beasts of burden, where a farrier was stationed), or the Smallpox camp, on a small lake a mile west of Deer Lake in Section nine, where the plague of 1880 hit with devastating force.

As has been said, the buildings were somewhat standardized. The one which most concerned the men themselves was the bunk house. After the crude shelters offered the shanty boys, anything would be an improvement, even where the bunks were "muzzle loaders." Men in these places had to crawl into their sleeping spaces from the end, as if into a tunnel. This of course made it possible to house more men in the allotted space. A "snorting pole," such as was used to keep horses apart in the barn stalls, was often installed in the bunks as a divider to keep the men from disturbing each other while asleep.

As bosses began to provide better working conditions (without, one might add, any prodding from unions), the "breech-loading" bunks came into being. These were not quite up to Waldorf standards, either, but they were an improvement. The mattresses were hay-ticks—bed-sized envelopes filled with wild hay. Strangely enough, they were fairly comfortable, if the hay was fresh, and they provided warmth. The main drawback was a tendency to get lumpy (which lumberjacks never complained of, since once they hit the bunk they were too tired for anything but to fall asleep), and their natural function as a habitat for wild life. An unused bunk quickly became a hotel for mice, and when a new jack tossed his turkey on it, there would be a general exodus of squealing rodents. Although it might be expected that the hay was a fire hazard, there is no recorded instance of a bunkhouse fire from this cause or any other.

Eventually bunks evolved to the single metal-framed ones with cotton mattresses, and heavy wool blankets of horseblanket gray. Mattress covers, sheet-blankets, pillows and pillow cases were issued, also. Since it was up to the individual jack to keep his bedding clean, sometimes these were so seldom laundered that after one season they were hopelessly grimy and could be handled only by someone with a strong stomach and a ten-foot pole.

A certain pecking order was observed in the bunkhouse, based on job rank and seniority. A man's bunk was his, with its lumps and bumps adjusted to his own shape. Even the mildest-mannered man was aroused when he saw a newcomer's turkey on his bunk, in one camp. He walked to it, tossed the offending pack onto the floor, and lay down. "This is

MY bunk," he said.

Once the men went to camp in the fall, they were pretty well set for the winter. The crew got organized to the work, and fell to doing their jobs without too much distraction. For that matter, it was a small crime to quit or leave camp until the job was done, or spring break-up, unless a man was injured or disabled due to illness.

The important thing was to get the timber out of the woods. The work day was from daylight to dark, and every jack "tied into it" with all he had. By night, tired and hungry from the cold, after supper he drifted off to sleep without any problem. Young and hardy spirits might sit around the "deacon seats" yarning, playing cards, or enjoying what other entertainment there was, but a growl from one less wakeful would soon quiet them down.

Most of the talk was about interesting incidents and people they had met in the camps, or the conditions in the camps themselves.

Many of the men involved in earliest camps were solitary, unsociable men with a past that wouldn't bear close scrutiny. Such was Paul Fournier, who had killed two people; George Cyr, another murderer; Jimmy Sears; Archie Logan, and Robert Logan, who left North Dakota with the cops a mere moose-jump behind him, and escaped by tossing the bicycles of his pursuers into the river. It was best not to know too much about these men. But the men on the deacon seats could compare notes on Ten-day Kelly, a good cookee but with such a powerful wanderlust that the most he would stay on the job was ten days, after which he had to go on a drunk; or Paddy-the-Pig, an all-round man who would send wood to camp. Pine Tiger was as tough as his beastly name. Tamarack Slim was a nickname given to more than one man, including a teamster, but Foxberry Slim was a good camp foreman with a reputation for high production, and a good following. Jack McLeod was known around the country as a good man to work for. And so on. Foremen, cooks and camps got their recommendation by word of mouth, and a bad reputation (deserved or not) was hard to live down.

A lumberjack called "Sixty-six" was a clown around the deacon seats. When asked where he got his name, he replied that he had worked in sixty-six camps in one year, and received sixty-six pay checks.

Louie Smith, another man in the crew, was considered a little "odd," though a good worker. But his claim to any common sense at all was ruined when he was seen shaving with a straight razor so blunt he howled as he scraped and pulled out his whiskers. Sympathetic listeners asked if his razor wasn't perhaps too dull. "It can't be," he said through his tears, "I cut my toenails with it yesterday."

In a freemasonry where every man was decidedly an individual, my friend Bob Daubendiek stands out as the ultimate nonconformist. A classmate of mine at Forestry School, he came to the camps in the winter of 1936-37, when deep snow and stinging cold had most operations strapped, and jobs were hard to get. I was sorry not to have his company in the camp where I was employed, but his fame soon spread and I got reports on him, regardless.

To begin with, he was the one exception I ever knew to the rule that lumberjacks dressed in heavy wool pants and mackinaws. Bob came to the woods in riding breeches and laced boots, a stylish outfit at the time, but not the most practical for the job. Nevertheless, that was what he wore all winter (perhaps because that was all he had brought along). When the breeches got holes in the knees, he wore them anyway, unpatched, even though the temperatures were regularly thirty below.

That alone would have got him talked about, but there was more. He wore pajamas. This was unheard of in a lumber camp. Most lumberjacks had never even seen pajamas. In the chill of the bunkhouse, the crew hastily stripped off their outer clothes and leaped into their bunks, but not Bob. Chilled to the bone though he might be, he wouldn't compromise. So every night the men would hurry into their sacks, and lie there, every eye on Bob, to watch developments: would he actually put his pajamas on again tonight? And every night, oblivious to their lively interest, Bob would haul out his pajamas, and on they would go. I wouldn't be surprised to learn that there were bets on it. It says something for the kind of man he was, forceful and determined, that nobody ever mentioned the subject to him.

Steel John was another strong, tough man. When a logging bridge across a river was needed, John just waded into the cold water, late in the fall, picked up deadheads from the bottom of the river, filled them with stones to support the bridge stringers, and built cribs for the bridge. Another time, when a cat broke through the river ice, he jumped right in and hooked cables onto it so it could be hauled out.

Sometimes a man with a crime on his record was traced to camp. It behooved the Arm of the Law to exercise caution with such rugged miscreants, and most of them were aware of it. Seeing one such lawbreaker being marched out ahead of the lawman, charged with shining deer, a jack was moved to inquire, "Why did you walk him out ahead of you?" The lawman returned sourly, "That s.o.b. could shoot the eyes out of a bumblebee."

When someone had played a joke on another they all knew, that was good for a laugh. Mansel Saunders got ribbed unmercifully because, while swimming in his birthday suit in the river, he had taken fright and fled into a nearby cedar swamp at the approach of some ladies in a boat. The unkind cut came from his friend and fellow-swimmer (who was modestly attired in overalls for swimming), in detaining the ladies for a friendly chat while the mosquitoes had a good go at Mansel's tender, unprotected hide.

Some might while away the brief bunkhouse hours with tests of strength and skill, like tearing in two a deck of cards, or a Sears, Roebuck catalogue. One camp boss used to entertain his men by showing his strong back. He would lie with his head on one bench and his feet on another. Then, starting with the lightest man, he would have the men step up on his belly, in turn, progressively taking on the heavier men. When he felt especially strong, he would let the men jump up and down.

The crowning feat seems to have been the trick of bending horseshoes. One Billy Goffie from Superior, Wisconsin, is said to have excelled in this display of strength, coordination, and power of concentration. He would take a no. 6 horseshoe (large size), holding it firmly in both hands. Then, gathering all his strength, concentrating it in his shoulders, arms, wrists, and hands, he would twist the heavy iron around in a 360-degree circle.

Another such man, John Olson of LaCrosse, Wisconsin, assured me he had done the same thing many times. I have no reason to disbelieve him after working with him a few days. Assisting with some tree planting, John was irked when cattle got through a fence and began trampling the small trees. He gentled his way up to a good-sized yearling steer, and POW! struck him in the head with his fist. The animal was rightly dazed, and barely staggered off with the rest of the herd.

The true story of "Taulan-Antti" (Giant Andy) was likewise a legend on the deacon seats. After he'd logged his claim, he wanted to clear the big stumps. He found a spare rail along the railroad track; it was, he thought, exactly the right tool, so he carried it home. Sure enough, it served his purpose well. He'd raise the rail and ram with it under a stump, then with a block for a fulcrum he easily pressed the rail down, and out came the stump.

Railroad inspectors looking for the missing rail eventually got wind of Taulun-Antti's activities, and went to inquire. Antti said, "S'ure, I gotu haffit tat pik rrrail to lif out tem 'tumps." The skeptical inspectors asked for a demonstration, and Antti proudly obliged. Thunderstruck, the inspectors left him the rail and walked away laughing.

Some camps played cards; in others it was taboo. Having kibitzers watch your strategy from the top bunks discouraged cheating, and the poker games were sometimes continuous, with no money changing hands until the end of the season. Wrangling of any sort was a disturbance, and was discouraged. A few men might display special acrobatics, or sleight of hand tricks.

Story-telling was a common practice on the deacon seats when the men were in camp. Good story-tellers helped while away the idle hours, entertaining each other with true experiences and tall tales.

With the intense interest and admiration for brute power, it is no wonder that the folklore around Paul Bunyan developed. Robert Pike says he was unheard of among the loggers in the eastern pineries. From what I can find, he first evolved in the bunkhouses of Minnesota, when the chief yarners were French, with their Gallic love of exaggeration. Somehow, after the camp populations became heavier on the more stolid nationalities, who were used to an existence of "life is real, life is earnest," the stories died down. There are very few tales left that have not appeared in print.

It seems appropriate that Bemidji has the original statue of Paul, with his blue ox, Babe. They were built as a public service by Leonard Dickinson and his brother, with Paul facing Third Street, watching the jacks come in off the Third Street saloons headed for the log drive down the Father of Waters.

The lumberjacks also used their imaginations to tell greenhorns of the fearsome critters they were apt to meet in the woods. There was the side-hill gouger, who would strike terror in all hearts. Newcomers were told to beware, also, of the agropelter, said to lurk high in trees and drop limbs on the unwary. The shagamaw was another weird creature, part bear and part moose, which walked a quarter-mile on its moose feet and then switched, to walk the next quarter mile making bear tracks. It seemed to have got its habits from watching cruisers in the woods, for it took a step exactly a yard long, and made a square turn at each section corner. In winter there was the snow snake, which killed its prey like a boa-constrictor. It was hard to see, being white, with a blowhole like a whale's through which it blew snow to blind its prey, and an unlucky young man lingering too long in the woods of an evening would find the six-foot reptile winding itself around him and squeezing him to death.

Old timers even spoke with straight faces of the dread wild teakettle, identified by its loud hissing noise, or the dingbat. These were nuisances rather than dangers. The wild teakettle confused woodsmen by its tracks, like snowshoes going in opposite directions, while the dingbat was a sort of moose-with-wings that bothered hunters rather than lumberjacks: it seized their bullets in midair, and stole their gasoline.

One Tamarack Slim claimed to have been part of Paul Bunyan's crew. He bragged of having been Paul's bullcook, hauling water from Lake Superior until he bailed the big lake dry. As part of his woods costume, he wore a ladies' silk stocking (called a "shook") stretched over his head and ears, under his old felt hat.

Games were apt to be rough, and (again) aimed at embarrassing the newcomer. One, similar to the eraser tag game the kids played in school, was called "Hot Ass." The jack who was "it" bent over, and received a mighty swat from a rubber (heavy rubber-bottomed boot) wielded by one of his buddies. He then had to guess who had done it. If he named the wrong man, his reward was another swat. If he guessed right, the other took his place. It might be played fairly until an unwary greenhorn was "it." Then, no matter how he guessed, he was always told that his answer was wrong, and swat upon swat was administered.

Blanket toss was another sport. Tricks like "seeing stars through a coat sleeve" or "pinning a cup to the ceiling" (in which the victim got a faceful of cold water) enlivened many an evening.

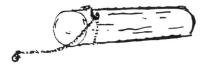

SKIDDING CHAIN ON LOG

Or there was "Buy My Sheep," in which a greenhorn was again hoaxed into being the butt of a joke. Two leaders led each participant, a "sheep" in turn to a spot beside a tub full of cold water, lifted him between them, and proclaimed him as "too light" or "too heavy." When the newcomer got his turn, the jokesters lifting him called out, "just right!" and dumped him into the tub.

Saturday night was maybe a time of music, if someone had a violin or mouth organ, and some rough-house dancing or jigging was done. Charlie Coolen, a good-natured woodsman, was noted for entertaining the crew with singing and dancing. Orin Patrow was as light on his feet off the logs as on, a tireless dancer, and in his rare moments of relaxation, a square-dance caller, singing out, "Heavy on the haystack, catty on the shoe pack—Tamarack 'er down!"

Some of the doleful ditties that were sung in the bunkhouse have come down to us, but few of them need to be repeated here. "The Big Rock Candy Mountain" was very popular. Swedes were partial to

"Nikolina," about a beautiful maiden whose parent lofted her suitor off the doorstep on the toe of his boot, and the rejected suitor was now marking time until the old man should die. Finns had a song to the tune of "Beautiful Ohio," sung in Finnglish:

Piki sika, piki sika, porkenpine
Stanting behint ta Norrrrvay bine
He look so 'lumpsy vit his hint feet behine
Piki sika porkenpine.

Piki sika, piki sika, porkenpine
Climpink so high in ta Norrrvay bine
I take my s'otgun and s'oot him town
Piki sika porkenpine.

I don't know any more of it, which is just as well. "Piki sika" may be translated as "pointed pig," or porcupine.

For a real oldie, Leonard Dickinson sings one called "The Little Brown Bulls":

Oh, the roads they were good and the timber was tall
To ten hundred thousand the contract did call
But mind you, my laddies, we'll keep your hands full
To skid in the woods with the little brown bulls."

Grand Rapids had its own song, about the Pokegama Bear. During the Depression, this lament was part of a cheerfully rueful song about life "on the bum" that seemed to strike the jacks as apropos:

I've topped the spruce, and worked the sluice,
And taken a turn at the plow;
I've searched for gold in the rain and cold
And worked on a river scow.
I've dug the clam, and built the dam,
And packed the elusive prune.
But my troubles hail, and I hit the trail
A-packin' my old balloon.

The bunkhouse sported a rack of poles at a convenient height, surrounding the stove. On this the jacks hung their wet socks to be dried for the next day, as well as their long johns and stag pants, if necessary. The effect this had on the air may be left to the imagination.

The creature who dealt most misery to the lumberjacks was the lowly bedbug, and the jacks despised him. Practically every log camp was infested with these smelly, vicious little insects with their unsportsmanlike habit of biting the jack during his off-duty rest. Somehow they always found their way to the camps, and raised hungry families who thrived on lumberjack blood. (Which, by the way, shows a certain amount of good taste: our local doctor told me that most lumberjacks had a hemoglobin count of *over* 100%). Kenny Tomlinson gave it as his opinion that the bedbugs multiplied so fast a bedbug born one morning was a grandmother within twenty-four hours.

The jacks waged war by boiling their clothes and blankets, and burning infested mattresses, but the miserable creatures laid their eggs in the crevices of the logs, and the moment a man relaxed, they were at him. The toiler would have his well-deserved slumber shattered by sharp, stinging bites, and in the morning would be decorated with puffy welts that itched like crazy and kept him scratching all day.

Sundays were "boil up" and wash days. Big iron kettles were used over outdoor fires to heat water where the men washed their clothes. This was the only way of getting rid of vermin, and it was only temporary.

Joe Danielson was a fellow who made life interesting around the camps. He was a wizard at throwing an axe. Many an unwary chopper looking around for his axe after Joe had passed by finally spotted it imbedded high in the top of a tree.

The Finns brought saunas to the camps. Most everyone in the camps got initiated, taking the "Finn baths" or steam baths eventually. Some men said this was their second bath in a lifetime—once in their mother's hands when a small child, and now steamcleaned in the sauna.

Except for the washing and personal chores, Sunday was a day of rest. In some camps it was possible to read a Sunday paper, though it did not necessarily reach the camp on that day. As a boy, Charles Bibeau made the rounds of half a dozen logging camps, pulled on a sled by his well-trained dog, selling the *Chicago Blade* and *Chicago Ledger*. The camps were several miles apart, and, to make his route, he sometimes had to stay overnight at one. His profit on the ten-cent paper was four cents.

Occasionally a traveling sky pilot came by and gave the men a spiritual uplift. Strangely enough, the hard-bitten rugged men had another side that could be tamed when properly ministered to.

Frank Higgins was the first of the dedicated men who sensed the innate decency of the lumberjacks, and spent years traveling from camp to camp. He was followed by his protege, John Sorenberger, who was even closer to the lumberjacks, having lived a rough-and-tumble past himself. He was a self-confessed thief, pimp, brawler, and murderer who had been pardoned by the Governor, thereafter giving his life to the rehabilitation of other troubled men.

Jacks respected these men for more than their message. Sorenberger was an ex-prize-fighter and Higgins was known to have used fists to subdue unruly drunks. But their main attraction was the speaking on their own terms, and singing. One lumberjack enjoyed this part of the program so much he said enthusiastically, "Goddamit, Parson, that's a damn fine tune. Let's sing 'er again."

"Okay," said the sky pilot, "We'll sing 'er again." And they did.

Not being able to understand all that was said didn't prevent the men's enjoying the services. After an evening of gospel hymns, one sky pilot asked for a raising of hands of all those who wanted to join him in Paradise. One blond giant did not raise his, and the preacher asked if he didn't want to go, too. "No," he said, shaking his head dolefully, "Ay tank ay go back to Nort' Dakota."

The work of Higgins and Sorenberger was carried on by Herbert Peters, whose dedication saw him through a monumental struggle. He started his career in the depths of the Depression, handling the farm delivery service for a store to help meet expenses while serving as a pastor to the churches of Bigfork and Effie. Many times, he got stuck in mudholes, hauling heavy supplies over poor roads, and carried the loads on his back, though he hardly weighed as much as the loads he packed.

During World War II, his work in the lumber camps was recognized, leading to a special mission assignment to the lumberjacks. His budget was meager, but he carried on.

Upon his arrival at one camp, he was told by the boss that there could be no services. "If you want to preach tonight, you'll have to go to Craig. The crew all went up there to celebrate the cook's birthday."

Inwardly frightened, Peters rose to the challenge and went to the lumberjack hangout, walking into the dive where the party was in progress. He stood in the doorway, and invited the men to go back to camp with him on his truck. At first there was silence. Then the men put down their drinks, and, one by one, followed him out. Back at camp, after coffee and lunch, Peters conducted services. From that time on, he had no fear that his work would fail.

Respect was nearly always given where respect was due. The Catholic Sisters, coming to the camps in pairs, never had cause to complain that they were badly treated or insulted in any way. The men were generous with their contributions to the poor, whom they somehow believed were worse off than they were. Sometimes the sisters had "hospital tickets." The purchase of a ticket entitled the lumberjack to hospital treatment if he should need it. Which he very well might. In a single month, twenty-eight lumberjacks were reported hospitalized in Grand Rapids, with broken legs, frozen toes, lung congestion, and other ailments, including "inflammation of the bowels" (now called appendicitis).

The cost of the ticket was usually a dollar a month, which was pretty fair from the sellers' standpoint. The men they insured were a husky, tough lot, who seldom had any ailments that required more than a dosing with horse liniment or a shot of whiskey. Most of the men who bought hospital tickets never needed them, which was probably something both sides were glad about. Those who did end up in the hospital got their money's worth and then some.

Nevertheless the jacks didn't always appreciate this forethought for their welfare. It's a matter of record that there was a lawsuit in 1902 over $3.75, when one lumberjack objected to seventy-five cents a month being deducted from his pay for hospitalization.

How it came out I don't know, but the law wasn't too much on the side of the lumberjacks. One dictum was that if a man accepted railway fare (hiring out in Duluth), he was obligated to work; wages of eight dollars a month were thought to be "high." The McCarthy law, that men must be paid when they quit, and not fobbed off with a time check until the timber was sold, met with opposition. It was charged that it made the men restless.

An idea of the schedule of the men who followed the timber can be gleaned from Fred Peloquin's journal of 1922. That year, he went to camp on December 5. A spate of illness hit him on December 21, so he went home, remaining there until after Christmas. Back in camp on the 27th, he stayed put until he cut his leg in a woods accident. This laid him up at camp until February 12. He started work again, only to leave on March 10 when camp broke up. Six weeks later he was building wanigans, accepting a consignment of peaveys and pike poles, and getting ready to take down a drive.

The unrelieved monotony of week after week of camp life must have made any unaccustomed face welcome.

Another visitor to the camps was William Nesbitt, a jeweler, who bought a trained sled dog from Jim Knight and made the rounds of the camps selling watches. Lumberjacks seldom had cash for such purposes, but they could be charged (on the "wanigan" or "van") against the man's earnings.

Though most of the crew's free time was spent in the bunkhouse, the cook shack was more important in their calculations. In the old days, board was provided, and included with the wages paid the men. In due time, as wages increased, all other costs naturally increased proportionately, until the cost of running the big camps became a problem to contend with. Charges for board had to be made, at first fifty cents a day, raising to a dollar by the 1930's.

The old-time lumberjacks were well fed, with the fare simple but nutritious, very much the same as was available in the homes of the time except more of it. Supplies of wild moose meat and venison were often the staples of the early logger. Beef, ham, bacon, and salt pork were toted long distances. Cookshacks housed large stocks of coffee, tea, salt, sugar, spices, dried beans, peas and corn meal, oatmeal, flour, and canned milk, along with molasses, dried apples, prunes and raisins.

The large company farm camps raised potatoes, rutabagas, onions, and cabbage, usually stored in root houses which were sometimes attached to the kitchens. Hogs were also raised at these camps, to be salted or pickled in barrels. Occasionally the gardeners put up home-made sauerkraut.

SKIDDING TONGS ON LOG

A typical camp menu might be as follows:

Breakfast—Sourdough pancakes, stacked high. Every cook kept his own "starter brew" going in a small barrel or crock. Oatmeal or corn-meal mush, with molasses poured on to suit the taste; Ham, bacon, or fried pork, with the fat used for buttering the cakes. Dried fruits were made into a stew, and fried potatoes were a staple. The breakfast drink was usually coffee, with cookies and doughnuts always on the table.

Dinner (the noon meal)—at the camp, or served by "swingdingle," a sled on which the cookees hauled food to the men in large pots, kept snug in blankets so that it was piping hot when it reached them: meat stew or mulligan, baked beans, sourdough bread and doughnuts (some cooks used sourdough in all the pastries). And pie, huge wedges, with tea or coffee to wash it down.

Supper, served at the day's end—Roast or fried beef or wild meat, baked or boiled potatoes with gravy, pea soup, baked beans (again), doughnuts, fruit sauce, pie, coffee, or tea. Occasionally butter, cheese, or eggs. The logging season corresponded to the time of year when animals didn't produce, which meant that eggs and dairy foods were available only in the preserved state.

Though the heavy high-energy winter food was satisfactory, by spring the men hungered for a change in diet. Many took to the woods and found wild onions, celery, mushrooms, and other wild plants and herbs. It was part of woods lore to know these plants. Jack Molan, working on line, showed me where mushrooms were carpeting the forest floor. He picked both his hat and mine full, and raced back to camp with them; so that our supper that day included the best cream-of-mushroom soup I've ever eaten. In summer, wild berries were in abundance. The cookees might spend an afternoon in the berry patch. Blueberries grew prolifically after cutover pine slashings were burned, and made especially good pies. Wild plums, cranberries—we found a patch of blackberries at one old farm camp that were delicious, and appeared to have been planted. Wild onions were thought to relieve colds, and, on log drives, some men ate them wherever they found them.

The cooks did miracles with what they had. They might not have known a good deal about nutrition, but they were well aware that you could move more timber with beans than with cake.

As transportation got better, so did the variety of foodstuffs, along with improved cook shack facilities. Lumberjacks rarely complained—but then, who would complain of choice moose stew, or venison roast, or braised ribs, or fresh walleye for dinner? I believe they had it better than we did later.

The old-time cook was the lord of the camp, and a law unto himself. Without a good cook you had no camp or crew to speak of, and well he knew it.

Because cooks were such martinets, it was a sporting proposition to try to outwit them. Cal DeLaittre tells that in one camp, high-spirited young jacks who enjoyed the cook's pies kept snitching whole pies that he had set out to cool. The irate cook finally got even. He put a filling of ox manure in them. The delectable top crust gave no indication of the actual contents, and this batch of pastries disappeared on schedule, but it's doubtful that the guilty grabbers took more than one bite. It's also doubtful that they ever stole that cook's pies again.

One memorable cook was Spike Patrow. He was jovial and witty, but not long-suffering. One gyppo contractor who hired him was verging on bankruptcy, a bit of hard luck that occasionally happened in spite of hard work. Seeing the handwriting on the wall, and having meager supplies, Spike took action. After feeding breakfast, he went about preparing dinner, whistling cheerily. Presently he informed the cookee, Emil Rylander, that he had business elsewhere, and couldn't stay to serve dinner. Emil's instructions were to keep the fire going, and to check on the big stew kettle on the stove at eleven o'clock.

At the appointed hour, Emil lifted the lid. The stew kettle contained the day's unwashed dishes, and, on top of them, an alarm clock. The dinner that day was alarm clock stew.

Cooks took no guff or nonsense from anyone. Generally they carried a cleaver, to restore law and order when things got rough, but most were not so grouchy as one extreme case. When a loud, noisy timber beast, returning from a wild spree, set up a fuss at the table, the cook reprimanded him. The jack then attacked the cook, which was a mistake: he received a swing of the cleaver on his neck. He never tried that again—he died.

During the Depression, a cook in a small twenty-man camp ordered a case of eggs. The boss, unfortunately, could afford only a dozen eggs. When the cook saw the pitiful supply, he hit the ceiling. A dozen eggs, he snarled, would be useless for baking, let alone feeding eggs twice a week. The boss suggested special economy—couldn't the cook use only one egg in a batch of doughnuts or a cake? With a look that would stun a rhinocerus at thirty yards, the cook grabbed a couple of eggs and smashed them on the stove. And the boss said never a word.

Stutterin' Frank Smith not only cooked, he cooked in all circumstances, and cooked well. The men said admiringly he could "make a good meal out of damn near anything." I remember seeing him making stew for log drivers, over an open fire. In the camp, he liked things clean, and his bullcook, Tom Brady, forced to carry water up a godawful hill, was moved to complain. "Howcome you hafta scrub these goddam floors so goddam often?" he grumbled.

Frank turned on him. "I'll scrub 'em three times a day if I hafta," he said, "and you'll carry the water." Which settled that.

Frank did lose his patience, though, as wanigan cook near Rice River rapids, and took off for town. The boss, Vic Lofgren, saw him hiking over the hill, and yelled, "Where're you goin'?"

Frank never slowed or turned. "I'm goin' up town—where the hell you think I'm goin'?" he yelled back.

"What's the matter?" Vic demanded.

"The goddam dough sticks to my fingers!"

In a small camp, where the homesteader's wife was often the cook, a man might fare very well, like one of the family. Sometimes besides the regular meals, lunch was brought to the men morning and afternoon, with a bedtime snack besides. There was seldom much turnover in these situations.

A camp that had a lot of "home guards" (local men) was presided over by a Swede cook with one eye and a wooden leg. This may not have been the reason the grub was poor, but whatever it was, a jack called "Sixty-six" felt it had terrible effects. *"Di aat aa den der maten saa di var aldeles bruns i oger na,"* he said: "The men ate that grub until their eyes were brown."

The early cooks went into the woods with the camp-building crew and stuck with it until after the spring drive. This may have been partly because, once there, they had no comfortable alternative. Later, when it became easier to get to town, cooks in the various camps began a sort of round-robin that resulted in a camp having a change of cooks fairly often, as one departed to the fleshpots to be replaced by another just coming off a prolonged drunk.

Dave Brown was one of the old school. "Thirteen-month Brown," he was called, though admittedly he did not always manage to live up to this virtuous name. He was very much a company man, as all old cooks were, and scorned "newfangled" ideas that would "spoil" the men. When a crate of lettuce was brought to our camp, he tossed it contemptuously into the kettle and served it boiled to a gelatinous mass.

He prided himself on gauging the efforts of the crew, and considered himself privileged to adjust their menu accordingly, going all-out to serve huge and tasty banquets when he thought the work was going well, and scornfully handing out run-of-the-mill grub when in his opinion the men had earned nothing better.

He stalked with an eagle eye among the tables at meals, observing when some staple was getting tiresome. "It's backin' up on 'em," he'd say in a conspiratorial growl out of the corner of his mouth.

A full larder was his pride "Ol' Dave ain't starvin'" he'd say with a leer, showing off his stores. But he was never one to admit a mistake. On one occasion, when he was bleary-eyed and hung over, the potatoes came to the table black and gummy. We were morally certain that Dave had grabbed soap powder in place of salt, and doused the spuds liberally, but Dave wouldn't take the blame. He wagged his head accusingly. "Somethin' wrong in that last batch of spuds you brought. But I kin fix 'em. Leave it to me," he said. And sure enough, the rest of that batch of potatoes were mealy-white and tasty.

Almost everything he cooked was done professionally well, but occasionally, when just back from a toot, he found it necessary to keep his coffee-can spittoon handy. The men came to view this habit with a sort of queasy horror, and refused to eat anything prepared at such times with "raisins" in it, on the principle that this might be a disguise for a slip in Dave's aim. Also, at such times he became disgustingly maudlin, reciting a long aggrieved history of his blighted romance, which, to hear Dave tell it, was no fault of his own.

One of the best we ever had, especially in a big camp, was Leland Nordahl. He was never happier than when he had a flock of cookees scurrying to do his bidding. The food he produced was mouth-watering, with flaky pastry, and a mustard sauce that was famous throughout the industry. He was a big, imposing man, scrupulously neat, with a dignity that did not unbend even in the presence of the Big Boss. Even when carousing, he was a man that no one approached with familiarity or foolishness.

This afforded quite a contrast to little JP, also called Snoose John, or Stutterin' John, who was probably one of the prime movers in the musical-chairs phase, being a jovial soul who liked a sociable chat, and a sociable drink even more. There was nothing wrong with his cooking, but he displayed a sort of nervous agitation that always gave way to a craving for a good bender. He could never last the season at any camp. One day the men would come in for supper, to find the cook had flown. His p-p-pies were popular, but his c-c-coffee was so powerful you could form it into a ball.

J P never came off a drunk without providing himself with the wherewithal to start another one, which he concealed in ingenious places. I recall one occasion when he had a kettle on the stove, half-filled with boiling water, in which there bubbled merrily three or four bottles of beer. When asked what was going on, J P looked innocent and harassed. With chattering chin he got out the words: "B-b-boiled b-b-beer is good for a c-c-cold."

Adam Smetko was nobody's sweetheart. He glared even when he smiled, which was seldom, and didn't look like he meant it the few times he tried it. His standard menu was a stew, so liberally spiced with whole peppers that it would lift your scalp a good inch with the first spoonful. So fierce was his expression, as he stood in his domain with cookees falling over themselves to avoid his disapproving eye, that no one ever complained, and he used that recipe without varying it throughout a whole season. He was also fond of padding his time card, and when Art looked at it with a snort and ordered the clerk to pay him only for such hours as he could reasonably have worked, got out his pistol and went gunning for the clerk (who fortunately was not at home). As might be expected, he didn't take kindly to suggestions. Norman, my brother, gave an unflattering opinion of one of Adam's concoctions, and Adam pulled a gun on him, ordering him out of the cook shack.

Most cooks were likeable fellows, and the bosses usually accepted their failings with philosophy and spoke fondly of their merits, but I never knew anyone who felt buddy-buddy about Adam.

The cook was lord of his domain, and woe be to any who crossed him. They all seemed to live up to their responsibility for plenty of nourishing grub, with as much bread and cake and pie as anyone wanted. There was coffee at any hour of the day, and sometimes at night, too, when a suddenly-shortened season forced night hauling. Most cooks considered themselves part of the outfit, and pitched in with unquestionable loyalty when anything which might have been considered beyond the call of duty was required.

They were jealous of their reputations, and allowed no adverse comments on their skills. Sometimes a man would leave a camp, and give as his reason that he "didn't like the cook," but that was seldom the truth; more likely than not he was spoiling for a drunk, but didn't want to admit it.

They permitted no chattering at meals. Such talkative behavior was discouraged by the cook's stalking around the tables. The most lengthy remark anyone was allowed to make was, "Pass the butter." The cook's motto was "Eat it, and beat it" so that his work would not be delayed by idle conversation or "cookshack logging."

The bosses, realizing that a good cook was beyond price in keeping a happy and ambitious camp, went all out to pamper these primadonnas and humor their egos. The cooks responded by keeping order in their domains and giving their best to the job. The cook shack was not a self-supporting accessory. In spite of the deduction for board from the men's wages, it was not expected to be. It was an accommodation that made all the difference between a satisfied crew and a disgruntled one. Bosses admitted it was worth going in the hole for board to keep good men. This demand reached its apex in World War II. My brother Art remarked in exasperation that the men then weren't willing to be satisfied with anything less than hummingbird's tongues.

It was discovered early that women cooks, unless they were married to a large and fierce lumberjack or to the boss, were nothing but trouble. Further, they were seldom equal to the demands of camp cooking—long hours, heavy utensils and implements, immense quantities, and the juggling of varying heats on the huge wood ranges, plus maintaining a proper master-and-slave relationship with the cookees and bullcook. There was seldom an overt problem, for lumberjacks invariably were respectful of women, and even shy around them, but in some indefinable way an unattached woman was a hazard to the camp's equilibrium.

Cooks preened themselves on certain delicacies, and sought praise as eagerly as a naive child. One man we had lamented that his skill at fancy cakes and decorated pastry went unused; another was constantly pointing out the superiority of his salad dressings. "I use Missoula oil," he stated with pride.

Whatever the trimmings, meat cookery was the foundation. Fresh meat was supplied in huge quantities, and stored in screened cool rooms. The early camps took care of the meat problem by having camp hunters—men whose job it was to keep game on the table. Occasionally a good farmer-hunter with an excess of game could sell something to the camps. The fee scale was not exorbitant: Lon Powell was paid ten dollars for a moose, and five dollars for a deer. Considering the dressed weight of a moose at 400 pounds to 500 pounds this was an inexpensive way to feed the men. Lon's part was done when the animal was field-dressed; he would blaze a trail for a man with a horse and dray to bring the meat to camp. The saloon keeper Hank Findley supplemented his salary by selling game to the camps. John Langhausen, a lad orphaned at the age of twelve in the Bear River country, got a job as cookee in a Namakan camp and was a meat hunter in his spare time. The skill he acquired then, when it was a matter of his bread-and-butter, stayed with him so that in his later years he had a Kodiak bear and a polar bear as trophies.

Hunting a moose was more of a science than one would think. An expert hunter, Fred Peloquin, gave me these directions:

When you come upon a moose while hunting, and jump him without being able to fire a shot, or even if you do fire a shot and he runs into the dense woods, a good hunter knows that he should run as fast as he can a quarter-mile or thereabouts on the moose track. At that distance he must become very alert, for the moose, thinking he has outdistanced pursuit, will stop to relieve himself, not suspecting that the hunter would follow so rapidly. Invariably you'll have a chance to fire at him.

Two men hunting moose, or three, increase their chance of success by signalling in whistles, while one tracks the moose, and the other follows on the downwind side. Using whistles, the tracker shows which way the moose is turning.

The cook's helper was known as a cookee. At times he was an apprentice cook, but more often it was an inside job handed to someone too young or too indolent to face the rigors of heavier work. He peeled potatoes, stirred soup, and did all manner of chores in meal preparation. During the meal he served as a waiter, keeping the dish-up pans filled. Then the clean-up fell to his lot, with the table being set immediately after, each dish upside down, cup atop plate. If dinner was served in the woods by swingdingle, that was his job.

Mike the Cook told me of a cookee who had an uncanny habit as he rattled the tin cups and plates into the proper place for every man on the long tables. According to some indexing of the character of each man as he saw it, he had a matching plate and cup with certain distinguishing marks or scratches on the tableware. Mike was rather dubious of this claim, but another cookee who had observed the process proved it after a series of checks on the table setting for the day. Mike paid a dollar on the bet, but in discussing it we came to the conclusion that the cookee was a brilliant wizard in modern psychology.

A fixture in the camps was the blacksmith, and he was an iron man in more ways than one. Besides the business of fashioning from iron any tool or piece of equipment the operation demanded, it was his responsibility to shoe the oxen and horses.

Shoeing oxen was a special problem. It had to be done in a special stall. An oxhide with holes for the ox's feet was first spread under the animal, then brought up around him, and fastened to a hand-powered log roller or windlass used to raise the ox's feet off the ground. Suspended in this manner, the ox could not kick or fight while being shod.

The shoe for the ox was smaller and simpler than that used for horses. Being cloven-hoofed, the ox required two half-shoes. Bob Prather, logging near Deer Lake, found fifteen ox shoes in a pile of debris, evidence that large numbers of them had been part of the operations there in the 1880's.

PEAVEY AND CANT HOOK ON LOG

The office was generally small, but vitally important. Here is where the clerk held sway, with his "van" and the medical kit. The term *van* usually referred to anything the camp might have for sale, as an accommodation to the crew; warm clothing, especially chopping mitts and liners; tobacco; files. No money usually changed hands on these transactions. The item was charged against the jack's wages until settlement was made in the spring.

Common medicines were available for purchase—the most popular of which were epsom salts and horse liniment. The horse liniment was considered as good for a lumberjack as for any other beast. One jack bought out the van's total stock of Jamaica ginger, a concoction with a high percentage of alcohol.

One staple in the clerk's van was snuff. This was also known as snoose, Norwegian dynamite, or Norwegian candy. Just why it was so popular would be hard to say. Perhaps it toughened the men, who could endure any pain if they could stand the snuff; or perhaps it anesthetized them. Maybe it even supplied that extra "push." One thing is sure, it was a necessity.

It came in quart-sized and gallon-sized ceramic jars which are a treasured find of collectors who probe the old ghost-ridden campsites. Oddly enough, the tops are seldom recovered. Perhaps the explanation is that when a Scandihoovian lumberjack opened a jar of snuff or a bottle of whiskey, he just tossed the top away and emptied the container before he put it down.

The office had bunks in it for the clerk or checker, the scaler, and the foreman, in the rear room. Stores and records were in the front room, with access controlled by a gate.

The clerk's duties were multiple, and defined somewhat by the size of the camp. As checker, he had to count up the logs and pulp cut by each individual jack, since pay was based on production. Understandably this sometimes led to mayhem, when his count and that of the cutter didn't agree. One checker was knocked cold by a protesting lumberjack over a difference of four sticks of pulp—but then the walloper had to use up his own coffee to help the wallopee clean off the blood from his face and clothes before going home to his wife.

The clerk was responsible for all records, so he checked not only the cutters, but the haulers as well. In tallying the loads, he held an outsize pencil in mittened hands, and was known to help with the loading on occasion. Success at the job called for adaptability and resilience along with an observant eye and knowledge of grading. A man of my acquaintance, new on the job, found this a little baffling. He had orders to get some pulp loads out first thing, then do some checking, while the boss went off to town. The man arrived in town shortly after the boss, much to the latter's surprise.

"What are you doing here? I thought you were checking."

"I am," said his new employee. "I'm checking out."

The crew respected his superior aptitude with works and figures, though the stupidest of them could figure to the gnat's eyebrow exactly what they had coming. As such he was held to be an authority on some matters not exactly in his province. For instance, one clerk in a Hurd and McAvity camp burned down the office when a dose of medicine he was brewing for a sick horse exploded.

The clerk was the boss' surrogate, and bosses usually relied on their clerks implicitly. This was not the case in larger operations, however. To prevent any hanky-panky, padding of payrolls, and the like, clerks in such cases could issue only time-checks, which were presented at the main office to be exchanged for actual checks. It was also customary to deduct for hospitalization insurance, with the first period's cost coming from the first day's pay. This pretty nearly caused a battle, when one jack, deciding to leave a camp after just one day's work, found that his net proceeds after the deduction came to something like ten cents. The clerk had no power to alter it and nearly lost his scalp over it, though it was of course adjusted at the main office.

The foreman, who also bunked in the office, was a natural diplomat who was responsible for everything and everybody. Old time foremen often held their jobs through the power of their fists. Theirs was the final authority, and when a disciplinary problem arose, it was up to them to find the solution.

Robert Pike tells of a case where a foreman even performed surgery. What appears to have been a circumcision was done without anesthetic (two men held the unsuspecting subject's legs) and with tobacco as a sterilizer. What's more, the operation was successful and the patient was grateful.

Such drastic remedies were seldom used. It was far simpler to haul the injured or seriously ill back to civilization. What was most needed was a sure-fire cold remedy. A favorite one sometimes used was a tablespoon of turpentine in a cup of hot water. Others improved the prescription by adding the turpentine to a cup of brandy. Many swore by horse liniment as the cure for anything, swallowed in liberal gulps or rubbed on a sore place. Otherwise, it was recommended to get good and pickled on the strong spirits, and by the time the hangover was over the cold was gone.

Little needs to be said about the bullcook, usually a has-been who carried out the camp chores. He'd now be called a maintenance engineer, but in his time he was usually called many another much less flattering name. Get wood—get water—keep those fires—swamp out this place— was the refrain he listened to all day long. It was no job for a lazy man. Sometimes a fine old fellow long past his prime as a lumberjack found it a haven in the years before social security, and made of it a bigger job than it had to be. I'll always remember old Matt Huotari's ceaseless rounds, stoking the fires in the immense barrel stoves, staggering into the cookshack under an enormous load of wood, shoveling paths that were like boulevards. I don't recall ever seeing him sit, except in the evening.

The lowly status of the bullcook made him the natural butt of bunkhouse jokes. One greenhorn on the drive fared no better. The drivers entertained themselves at his expense by warning him about the vicious bullcook lice. Drivers themselves, they earnestly swore, were immune to these voracious creatures, because, being wet constantly, they had no scent. The ravening bullcook lice could smell only the bullcook, and made a beeline for him and his bunk.

The fearful bullcook spent many an anxious moment shaking out his bedding, inspecting his underwear, and sniffing his underarms. In due time his vigilance was rewarded.

One driver found an enormous water beetle, so huge he could barely fit into the Copenhagen snuff can in which he was placed for safekeeping. At the proper time this insect was released into the bullcook's bunk.

The eruption that followed would make Mt. St. Helen's explosion seem like a falling angel cake. Sufficient be it to say that it was the only bullcook louse that luckless innocent ever saw. He never went on a drive again.

When camp closed down, if supplies remained, a watchman usually stayed in the buildings to keep an eye on things. Frank Werthner stayed on when Quinn Camp no. 5 moved out everything but some brood sows that had been left to his care on the place. He also had a secret pet—a horse which had been slightly injured in a sluicing accident, and thus escaped the fate of the other forty head of horses from the camp. Glanders had infected the herd, and all of them had been destroyed, at the spot which has since that time had the gruesome name of Dead Horse Rock. The crippled horse, not being with the others, had been forgotten in the slaughter, and was recovering from its wounds. Frank discovered the animal, a beautiful, gentle horse, and began to carry oats out to it. The horse seemed perfectly well, with no sign of glanders, and Frank began to make plans to take it home with him.

But it was not to be. One day a man came, sent by the authorities, with orders to find the horse and shoot it. Frank pleaded for its life. "Why don't you tell 'em you shot it?" he begged. But the man had a job to do, so finally Frank told him where to find the horse. Telling of it sixty years later, tears came to Frank's eyes, and he wept.

Watchmen were needed to protect the camp from animals rather than men. Alone in the timber, a man might have no defense if he encountered a hungry predator. There were many stories of pursuit by wolves, though I know of no authenticated case of their killing a man. Perhaps they just didn't leave any evidence.

Bears were a constant source of trouble, spring and fall, during all the logging era. We built the screened meat houses with extra heavy two-by-four studdings a foot apart, and cross-braced on the inside, for protection against their invasions. Certain bears seemed determined to break in, almost as if it were a sporting proposition to not be thwarted in their attempts.

One cook was nearly hysterical when a very persistent bear attempted to rip the door off its hinges. He pushed everything he could against it. The bear, foiled at his attempt at easy entry, walked the entire length of the cookhouse roof sniffling and growling, with the cook cowering and gibbering in the farthest corner.

A lean and hungry bear gets more daring, and one spring, such a bear kept pestering the cook. He tried valiantly to shoot it, but his aim was poor. Either the bear would have to go, or the cook would, so I had to take action. It was easy to track the animal back from the cook shack, for the bear had a missing toe. I was following its trail, when suddenly I looked up and saw the bear coming towards me, about ten yards away. I broke all records sprinting for the cook shack. Old Dave, seeing me running, met me at the door with the rifle, and I turned and shot the bear, standing twenty yards away. That finished his depredations.

I'd thought of having a bear rug to commemorate my outrunning the bear, but it was impossible. The poor animal was so covered with wood ticks he was untouchable.

A bear who added insult to injury visited the trailer of a watchman in an isolated area. The man had made an early Saturday trip to town for supplies, and on returning to his trailer, had left his purchases in his trailer. He then made the rounds of the equipment for several hours.

As he approached the trailer, his little dog began to bark excitedly, and he saw that his trailer door was open. Inside was a shambles—his supplies were mangled and scattered, the meat and butter were gone. What was worse, the bear had lain down on his bed and taken a nap.

He cleaned up the mess in some annoyance, repaired the door, and replenished his supplies.

Next morning, as he was making coffee, he felt the trailer being jolted. Simultaneously his dog began barking wildly at the door. As the man looked, the bear tore loose the bottom of the door, bent it upwards, and thrust his head into the opening, jaws opening in a maddened roar. With the dog snapping at the bear's nose, the man ran for his rifle. Luckily he didn't miss.

The noise of axes and saws, and later the various engines, generally kept wild animals from bothering the men at work. The most they usually had to report was a fleeting sight of one, though a lynx once invaded our blacksmith shop. But the forest animals were not to be trifled with. If I had a choice, in the woods without a gun, I'd rather meet the agro-pelter.

Lumberjacks accepted their life without women without complaint, though I do recall one old shacker asking wistfully if someone wouldn't find him a "long-haired partner—any of them there hollow-butted windfalls" to come and share his diggin's.

One very unusual story was told by the teamster Billy Tell. He worked all winter with a willing skidding helper, Jackie, and they had a most cordial relationship as bunkmates. In the spring, he was surprised to meet Jackie in town dolled up in the finest. Jackie was a pretty lady! Billy was still dumbfounded telling about it thirty years down the road. Perhaps many of the young and old jacks dreamed of such an opportunity, but never had any such luck.

In fact, long hours of demanding work may have brought about the very opposite. When Martin and McGraw went to bed quarreling, McGraw awoke to find Martin trying to cut his throat, and barely escaped with a slashed ear. A morose young worker only thirty years old committed suicide in a sixteen-inch water hole. Swede Charlie tried suicide by diving under a logging train, but he tripped and was saved.

Other hazards might beset a man, especially one working alone. Cruiser John Gilmore cut his leg to the bone with his axe. Keeping his cool, he used his belt for a tourniquet, cut all the brush within reach for a wigwam, and when help did not arrive, dragged himself out at the rate of three miles a day in weather of ten degrees below zero. Chopper Bill Smith was lost for thirty-six hours, and badly frozen. A W Lewis died when a falling limb crushed his skull. A man working with a geologist got separated from his gang, and was never found. A bear cut a swath through a lumberjack's clothing; a man reported being surrounded by wolves who followed him home; a note was found left by a man who knew himself to be dying of fever, who had fired his last shot for help in vain. Morris McKinney died of appendicitis, Frank Munson sluiced his load, got run over, and was picked up dead. And there was smallpox. Year after year new cases would be taken to the pest house. Not until after 1900 was the practice of burning smallpox camps deemed unnecessary. Records show that a lumberjack was fined for jumping quarantine in 1902. Lumberjacks survived all these and many more dangers in the battle to get out the timber.

Injuries became less frequent in the woods as safety practices grew more widespread. They were also less likely to be serious, and hardly ever fatal. Perhaps this might be the time for me to pay tribute to men

I remember in our employ who died, not in logging accidents, but while they were part of a crew: Oscar Kilmer, drowned while chauffering an importunate group of jacks to town, much against his inclination; Grandpa Will, crushed by a wayward lumber load; Albin Hanson, dead of a heart attack; Big Emil, frozen in his car; Eddie Anttila, burned to death in his shack from a carelessly-left cigarette; Tom Blacker, lost somewhere in the woods, depressed and unhappy; and Dave Brown, whose heart gave out, found on the river bank where he watched the logs in the mill pond. Last but not least, my brother Bill, who died as he lived, and as he would have wanted to die, with an axe in his hand.

When there was a death in the crew, the men passed a hat and gave generously to the survivors. Then, subdued, they went on with their work. The logging had to be done.

Loading pine logs on a sleigh with a sidejammer. The man driving the cross-haul team hoists the log, while the top loader is ready to place the log. Much of the old style logging equipment was built by blacksmiths and woodbutchers right on the job. (Itasca County Historical Society)

9

All Work and No Play

When Paul's seven axe men headed for town, the saloon keepers boarded up their joints, and hid. They never forgot the time one of Paul's crew hit the bar with his fist and caused the San Francisco earthquake. Another time, one blew the foam off his beer and the wind of it took down a forty of timber.

I suppose people who study such things might say that the lumberjacks were the spiritual heirs of the Vikings, or ought to be. They certainly had the same ideas. They didn't think life was worth much if it wasn't tough. Nobody wanted to be a softie, and anybody who complained got jeered at. The old Vikings would rather fight than anything else when they were out for a good time, and their idea of Valhalla was a place where the men sat around on a prolonged drunk and continuous daily battle, while beautiful girls kept their mugs full. A lumberjack would be right at home in a heaven like that.

You could spot a lumberjack town by the raw, wild and free-wheeling atmosphere. Usually the sour mash and beer smell met you outside the door. The plank walks and the floors in the joints were scarred from the "corked" shoes, and rows of rough board and tarpaper shacks lined the streets.

Deer River was the jumping-off place for most lumberjacks headed up country for Bigfork and Effie camps, and Craig, the end of the line. A whole section of the town's main street was designated as "Whiskey Row," with plenty of saloons where they could while away their time and be relieved of their money. When they needed to recuperate, they could sleep on the floor of the Mohr Hotel, and take the next logging train back to the woods.

With the help of their buddies, most of them managed to make the train north when their money was gone. Usually they were herded into one coach, where they continued any brawls they hadn't had time to

Dinner out in the woods, delivered by the cook and cookee in the lunch sled or "swingdingle," more often delivered by a horse and cutter. (Itasca County Historical Society)

Jump starting a big sleigh load of logs. The luff team, attached to block and tackle on the side of the sleigh, assisted in getting the big load moving, then cut loose on the fly. (Itasca County Historical Society)

Drive boss Fred Peloquin and helper Bob Pederson preparing a charge of dynamite to blast a troublesome rock in the river that caused a log jam. (Ben Rajala Col.)

E.W. Backus' Int'l Lbr Co Wanigans on the Big Fork River. Backus was known to have good food on the log drives as well as the winter logging camps. (Ben Rajala Col.)

The water tank crew and team were an important part of logging operations. Icing the sleigh ruts made for easier movement of the big sleigh loads. (Itasca County Historical Society)

The "Steamhauler," as it was called, was a good example of the ingenuity of the pioneer loggers' ability to get the timber moving faster and cheaper. This was a forerunner of the modern crawler tractors or Caterpillars. (Itasca County Historical Society)

Matt Strom and Earl Peloquin (top photo, Ben Rajala Col.) were a fast pair of pine fallers. They sawed the logs that made up the historic load that stood near the Itasca County Court House for years (bottom photo, Itasca County Historical Society). The sleigh was top loaded by the notorious Sid Williams. It took six truckloads to haul the logs.

This was our last logging camp, used for thirty years (1947-1977). The men are coming to supper. (Ben Ragala Col.)

The last logs in the Big Fork River on their way to the Bigfork Mill, 1957. Ben Rajala and Art Rajala. (Ben Rajala Col.)

One of the big Bass Lake white pine skidded by Bill and Sven Rajala and four good horses. (Ben Rajala Col.)

Talk about doing things in a big way! They knew how in the old days. It would take ten big, modern trucks to haul this tandem load that one teamster and six good horses were hauling in 1909. (Ben Rajala Co.)

finish. Even if they were peaceable, the damage they did to the coaches was horrendous, spitting on the floor or on the closed windows when they aimed outdoors, ripping up the floors and seats with their boots, being sick in the aisle or spilling food or drink. Fights sometimes resulted in stains from bloodied noses, and wrecked furnishings.

It was enough to strike terror to the hearts of the incoming settlers. As a boy, A D Moors saw a sight he never forgot, when the train with several carloads of drunken lumberjacks stopped at a logging camp on the way to Bigfork. A man came reeling off, with blood spurting in all directions from a slit throat. Nobody paid any attention, except the wide-eyed boy. The train went on, and nobody bothered to see whether the man lived or died.

Deer River was wild and wide open. But rated X, right along with Saginaw, Muskegon, Hurley, and Portland and Bangor (back east where it all began) was Craig.

Craig, or Craigville, looked the part. The thirty-some odd buildings that lined its one-sided street were nearly all "blind pigs"—a term for a business that sold rotgut while pretending to be something else. Interspersed among the dens of iniquity and gambling joints, at a safe distance apart, were a couple of general stores, a depot, two hotels with "Good Eating Restaurants" for those who bothered stopping to eat, a sawmill and lumber camp, and Finn baths for boiling off a few layers of the winter's accumulated scale and crud.

Scattered among these were the lairs of the "maidens," one aptly named "The Big Ship" for dryland sailors and lumberjacks, where you could, if you had the money, buy everything that made Sodom and Gomorrah famous. Some of the notorious ladies occupying these premises (which Jack Molan referred to as "them Horizontal Recreation Parlors") had such names as: Ole Milly, Dutch Mary (who claimed the performance record in terms of quantity, comparing the numbers of her customers with the ties in Backus' railroad); Big Alice (who had whiskers, and talked rougher than most tough lumberjacks); There was Big Tit Tillie, Scarface Jean, Box-car Nell, Tamarack Lil—more than one of whom claimed to have given away a million dollars' worth before they knew it was worth money—along with many nameless broads and battle axes, one they even said must have been split with a broadaxe herself. They all came to offer romance or a reasonable facsimile thereof to the 4,000 to 5,000 lonely and sometimes woman-shy jacks who were on their way in from the woods, or the log drivers passing through. They came to Craig from other haunts, with quite a lot of mileage behind them. When the boom ended, they left for greener pastures, and may well be plying their trade along a skid row someplace. The last of 'em hung tough, handling the trade all alone from World War II until the bitter end.

Craig had other more potent attractions for the jacks even than the society of friendly ladies. That was the "moonshine" or rotgut booze that flowed freely, illegal or not, at all hours of the day or night, and the gambling for high stakes against the professionals who were always ready to relieve a man of his hard-earned stake.

If this had been all that went on in Craig, it would never have acquired the lurid reputation that it had throughout the years of logging. But it had two natural features, a hill and a river, that were made-to-order for the unscrupulous bloodsuckers who didn't mind a bit of robbery or murder if they could get away with it, even when there were such easy ways of getting the lumberjack's money in the open. It was no secret that men who stumbled up the hill to the bunkhouse with any money at all left were apt to be hit over the head with a blunt instrument and rolled back down, under the cover of darkness, there to be slipped into the river or pushed through a hole in the ice. Most of the time their bodies were never found. If they were, nobody inquired very far—a lumberjack was likely to be a man with no family and no known relatives. Inquiry for a missing man seldom came from Outside, unless he was wanted by the law or pursued by a deserted wife.

If the body did come to light, nobody got very excited. It wasn't unusual for log drivers to see a man's body surface in their working area.

When Charles Bibeau and his partner, a cheeful, happy-go-lucky, singin', whistlin' Tennesseean were poling logs from a jargo near Craig, a dead body popped to the surface between the logs. The Tennesseean froze from shock, in mid-whistle, and became sick. "I'm gonna quit," he said, shivering. "What kind of people is these, anyhow?" He finally compromised by getting stinking drunk, with such a terrible hangover the next day he was no use on the drive and was nearly drowned himself, unable to keep his balance on the jargo. As for the body, the coroner came and got it, and that was the end of the matter.

Even the children of the community were aware of the seamier activities. One spring morning, when the usual pair of students went to the spring at the river's edge, for water to fill the school's water-cooler, they noted what looked like a basketball bobbing along in the water. They waited for it to come within reach, so they could snag it for their playground fun. When it got close, they saw it was not a basketball after all—it was the back of a man's head, carried northward by the current.

How many men disappeared in this fashion was anybody's guess. Friendless, homeless men were never missed.

Not all killings were secret affairs. Grudge fights helped fill the burial grounds, too, and entertained the general population besides. The most famous was the duel between Cunningham and McGinty.

Both of these men were tough gamblers from Bemidji, working as house gamblers in two of the establishments. Some trouble arose between them—possibly it was just that the town was too small for two hot-shot gamblers, and there was not much business that winter.

At any rate, a run-in took place in the moonshine bar where the bartender was Cunningham's friend. He came to Cunningham's assistance with a stove poker, striking a mighty blow that bent the poker in the shape of a U. McGinty, cold-cocked, must have been part lumberjack—he was felled, but not knocked out. He got to his feet and left, but the next day he was back. He spoke coldly to the bartender.

"Go home and tell your wife goodbye," he said. "I'm going to get Cunningham first, and then I'll take care of you." He left the joint and went on up the hill, looking for Cunningham.

The worried bartender got word to Cunningham about the threat, and when McGinty returned, Cunningham was armed and waiting, standing sheltered by the end of the bar. Even so, McGinty got his shots off first. He fired wide, striking his enemy in the chest both times, in spite of the protection of the bar. Cunningham fell, but he got off one shot that dropped McGinty dead.

STAMP
HAMMER—
EDGLER BROS.

There were no repercussions from the law, but the party-line telephones really buzzed as the excited citizens discussed the latest commotion with a mixture of ghoulish glee and pleasureable horror. Most sympathy was for McGinty, who, though a tough ex-pug, was normally mild-mannered and would not hurt an ordinary person without provocation.

You didn't have to be a professional gambler to get into trouble with the card sharks. Bill Laine was a shrewd man with a deck of cards, and always hoped to double his winter's logging stake so he could send to the old country for his wife and daughter. He hit a winning streak, and came out of a game with a fairly substantial windfall. The word got around, and before he could leave town with it, he was shot in the street, and left for dead. Fortunately for him, he didn't die—but the hospital stay most certainly took care of any profit he might have made. Nobody was ever charged with the shooting.

Some of the businesses gave the jacks something for their money, but they were outnumbered by those who considered them scum who would never know what had become of their stake anyway, so jacks were fair game for any operator, fair or foul. Jim Stewart, an ex-logger himself, attempted to run a decent place. Along with his saloon, he kept some fine horses for hire. He had a customer of surly nature who had been drinking on the cuff too long, by Stewart's standards, and he demanded payment. The man refused. Stewart took his rifle, and shot the man dead. He surrendered himself to the authorities, who put him away in prison for the rest of his life.

When Prohibition was enacted, a town that was rough got even rougher. Presumably since the operators were outside the law to begin with, a little more crime wouldn't weigh very heavily on anyone's conscience. The town received a transfusion of cold-eyed freebooters, who feared nobody, dared to do anything that looked like providing a profit, and brazened it out in front of everybody except the "revenooer."

The federal revenue officers tried from time to time to do something about Craig, but it was a losing battle. To begin with, the nearest county agency for law enforcement was at International Falls. It was connected to Craig only by a very roundabout route on a commercial railway that took the better part of two days to get there, or a sixty-mile logging railroad. A friendly railroader could easily tip off the barkeepers and bootleggers, so that when the officers finally did pull off a raid, there was no evidence to be picked up. For their part, the bootleggers had an Early Warning System that was never fully revealed. When the Revenue Men were suspected of being in the vicinity, the wily operators had ingenious methods of breaking all the bottles of illegal "moonshine." Some of them had storage shelves in their cellars or back rooms that could be tripped by a rope attached. When the "feds" burst in the door, the bartender gave a quick yank; down went the shelf, and there went the evidence. Others had slides of one sort or another, or relied on their trusty hammer. The more philosophical or cynical ones let themselves be picked up from time to time, and hauled off to the judge, where they paid a fine (easily recouped) and added a little gratuity on the side to help keep nosy lawmen off their backs. This was considered a sort of civic duty and sometimes an insurance against bothersome raids. One lone Dick-Tracy type did arrest and line up a group who drove themselves to Bemidji in their own cars, paid their fines, and returned to business as usual.

The bartenders were always alert to avoid the raids if there was a sporting chance. Naturally they were suspicious of strangers. One man who arrived in a Cadillac, wearing a suit, appeared so obviously a high-ranking Federal man out for blood that the proprietors went into action on sight, smashing their bottles and dumping their wares. They were really mad when they learned he was a boss boot-legger, coming to give them a little competition.

One particular saloon keeper can serve as an example of the kind of men who gave the town its reputation. It has been said that in his later years he "got religion" so the deeds which were attributed to him had best not be remembered in his name. But it is interesting to note how many instances of rough brutality and downright skullduggery are credited to him by the men who passed through.

He ran a rough-and-tumble, knock-down-drag-out sort of saloon business, and was said to have got many a man's money when he was too befuddled by drink to know where it went. One eyewitness said he knocked a drunk Finlander down with a club, killing him, and then dragged him down to the waterhole in the river ice, from which water was dipped by some townspeople. (The river, by the way, was commonly used by many of the saloon keepers as the source of water for cooking or diluting the moonshine. Nobody seemed to ever worry about pollution.) The waterhole proved too small to shove the man through, and soon the tavern-keeper was seen running back with his axe to enlarge it, cursing all the time about his troubles. But the man was harder-headed than he had supposed. When the bartender got back, the Finlander was gone. He'd come to, and gone back to the whiskey row.

A watchman at Reid's mill happened into the place when things were pretty quiet. The saloon keeper was annoyed. "What the hell's wrong; nobody's buyin' drinks," he complained. "Can't keep this place open for you guys if you ain't buyin'." He looked at a dirty, unkempt jack slumped over the bar, in a drunken stupor. "Oh, Joe, here—he'll buy a round." Reaching into the man's pocket, he extracted the roll of bills that represented the remains of Joe's stake, and peeled one off. "He'll need that to buy a drink when he wakes up," he explained, and shoved it back into the man's pocket. The rest of the roll he took back to the till, and gave everybody a drink on the unconscious Joe. The men drank, but afterward agreed that it would be wise never to get drunk in that joint.

Taking advantage of lumberjacks was fairly easy, with the "banking" method the jacks used. When they hit town, they often handed their check to the first bartender they visited, with the understanding that anything they spent in his place was to be deducted from it, along with a small cash advance. That way, they reasoned, they wouldn't be risking that someone would kill them for the money they carried, as they made their unsteady way up the row of moonshine joints. From time to time, as they used up the advance, they'd come back for more money, until it was all gone. An honest bartender gave them all they had coming. A crooked one grabbed at the chance to siphon most of it into his own pocket, and frequently got away with it. A lumberjack on a toot could easily lose track of his spending, and he had only the bartender's word for it when he was broke.

This particular saloon-keeper was an expert at bullying the jacks and browbeating them into giving up the battle when he said they were out of money. The men might dispute his word, but they never got any money back that he didn't want to give them. There are two unimpeachable witnesses for one such event in his joint. One of them, Swan Freeberg, was a much-respected company foreman. He swore me to secrecy, telling me that if word of the story got out, he feared for his life.

It started out as the usual tale of the drunk making his boozy way up the street after depositing his check with the bartender. When he needed funds, he returned, half-shot, and asked for some of his money. The bartender swore some mighty oaths. "&#$!%$#$&X! you dirty bum, get out!" he said. "You haven't got any money. You've used it all. Now get out!"

PARBUCKLE WITH DOUBLE OR SINGLE SWAMP HOOK

Evidently the jack wasn't all that drunk. He swore furiously that he did too have money coming. He'd only taken twenty dollars, and should have several hundred left. The bartender had better hand it over, or else. He looked threatening. The bartender thought it over for a moment.

Well, maybe the guy actually did have some left, he said. He didn't think so, but maybe there was a mistake. He'd go in the back room and check the books. Meanwhile, here was a drink—and he placed a glass in front of the man. He disappeared into his back room, and the men in the bar heard the back door shut as he ducked out.

Moments later a rifle cracked. A bullet tore through the tarpaper wall and the man dropped to the floor, killed instantly.

Before the men around the bar had time to sort things out, the bartender came briskly in the back door and entered the bar.

"What the hell's happened here? Who shot that guy?" he demanded. No one knew, other than that a bullet had burst through the rough boards, and the man fell dead.

"You guys help me get him out of here," the bartender ordered. Some dazed customers helped him drag the body out back and cover it with snow, while the bartender mopped up the blood.

Swan Freeberg's story ended there, except that he added that he never again had a drink in that bar. He saw quite clearly what had happened. After placing the drink on the bar, the bartender went into his back room, picked up his rifle, and left by the back door. By counting the one-by-four slats on the building wall he knew exactly where the man was standing, drink in hand, and let him have it. Next day Swan went behind the building and checked it out. But when he told me this story, in 1938, he made it clear I was not to divulge it, even though it had happened nearly twenty years earlier. All those present had been threatened, if they ever talked.

The epilogue came from another witness. He said that the next morning, he and another man went to check on the corpse, to see if the victim could be identified. What they found was a trail to the river, showing where something heavy had been dragged. A clinching event took place in the spring. When log drivers reported finding the body of the man with a bullet hole in his back, the bartender shrugged. "Man! I never figgered anybody'd ever find, him, under the ice," he said. It didn't appear to rest heavy on his conscience.

Because Craig was known to be a hell-raising place, that's where the boys went when that was what they wanted to raise. Bartenders kept a certain amount of order to prevent their places from being demolished in drunken brawls, and usually had a blackjack, or something like it, handy, which they had no restraint about using. They didn't always figure to a nicety the exact amount of persuasion needed. One saloon keeper trying to subdue a noisy timber beast miscalculated his own strength. He hit him with a hatchet, through cap and hair, and the man dropped like a poleaxed steer, spreading blood all over the pine board floor.

The barkeep was a bit jolted. He hadn't meant to be that rough, and, anyway, a corpse on the floor was bad for business. He got a little nervous. There was one other patron at the time, one Tamarack Jack, whom he persuaded to drag the fallen man out to a snowbank to await later disposal. Tamarack Jack agreed to do the favor for twenty-five dollars, and he did.

Once he got the victim cutside, he realized he was still breathing. However, he reasoned it was no business of his, and he wanted to earn his twenty-five dollars, so he dragged the limp body to a snowbank and left him, returning to the tavern to finish his refreshments. He was still there later, when the door opened, and a swaying, bloody, wild-eyed figure entered the joint, heading uncertainly for the bar.

The saloon keeper took one look at the unrecognizable apparition, his hair matted, his face invisible behind a mask of blood and dirt, his clothes awry, dirty and sopping. Possibly he'd had a few snorts to steady his nerve. His eyes bugged out, he grabbed the bar with both hands, and began to shriek:

"Jeez! It ain't you—I killed you!" and when the Incredible Hulk kept coming, he bolted out the back door like a rabbit into its warren, never to return.

From all the stories about the denizens of Craig, it appears that many of the saloon owners were not really tough guys, but bullies who took advantage of men they would be afraid to meet in a fair fight. Joe Poliquin was different. He was not a big man, but well-built and quick. He never backed up from anybody if he thought action was called for. Joe was a merry and jovial-spirited fellow, not given to quarreling. He did barbering, and was a jack-of-all trades. When Prohibition was repealed, he had a liquor store and bar. His eyes were unlike any I ever saw, their color a cross between that of a rainbow trout and a speckled trout, that sparkled when he was up to some devilment.

He had a place in Effie where people gathered to play pool and enjoy late evening lunches. One night, after a show, I was there when the notorious Craig bully mentioned earlier came in. He had with him an old lumberjack, MacLaren, whom he was abusing. Several times he hit MacLaren, cracking him on the side of the neck and knocking him down. He was proceeding to kick the old fellow, when Joe ran up to him and struck him a good wallop in the solar plexus. "Get out!" he said, "And don't come back unless you can behave. If you bother that old man any more, you'll get worse." The bully turned and left without a word.

As a young man, traveling by train to Montana to see the Dempsey—Gibbons championship fight, Joe happened to meet Jack Dempsey in the aisle. Joe tossed his turkey on a seat, punched Dempsey in the belly, and stepped back quickly. "Haw-haw-haw!" he said. "I just wanted to see what it felt like to sock the world's champion!" For a second he was ready to run at the killer expression that crossed Dempsey's face, but kept his own broad grin in place. Dempsey relaxed, and they shook hands. It gave Joe a story he was fond of telling again and again. "Dempsey's belly was hard as a rock," he would say.

There were other people in the area near to Craig besides the riff-raff, and living with the flagrant vice and degeneracy did nothing to make their lives pleasant. One of these was Pete Wiegant, (whose name somehow came out "Wiggins" on the local tongues), the unkempt depot agent, who handled most communication with the outside world. Originally a first-class telegraph operator, he ended up in the lumberjack hangout as a kind of recluse. He was also the postmaster, and often delivered the mail to the various places along the street that were too busy to pick it up themselves. Being a bachelor with not too much skill in cooking, he liked to time these deliveries at mealtimes, so as to be invited to sit down to dinner. His was the only telephone in town. When someone came to use it, and thanked him for it, he would say sourly, "That won't buy any bread."

But he gave no support to the lawless element. The Reverend Herb Peters visited him once, in the company of a New York minister. They found him in his den, where he lived like a hermit, dirty and unshaven, in the old dilapidated Minneapolis and Rainy River depot in Craig. Pete rose to the occasion, offering them "coffee that's stronger than whiskey, but better for you."

Men who might otherwise have been decent, hardworking husbands and fathers succumbed to the effects of the rotgut that passed for whiskey in the joints. The citizens of Craig heard frantic screams at the river bank one spring day, and ran down to see what was happening. At the water's edge two people were struggling; a man, crazed by drink, was trying to drown his Indian wife, holding her head in the water, while she fought with all her strength to escape.

Hardened though they were to violent deaths, the case of one bootlegger caused a feeling of horror to spread throughout the north country. With his wife and three small children, he was living in a shack near Craigville, while working in the woods. Unfortunately, he was spending a good bit of his time and pay in the dives.

The poison of the raw moonshine worked on his brain until something snapped. He grew moody, morose, unpredictable. Coming home one day in a mindless fury, he seized his wife and slashed her throat. He did the same to their infant son. The little girl fled from the shack in terror, and the wife, horribly cut and bleeding but not dead, staggered out and hid in the woods with her crazed husband in pursuit. She eluded him, and finally made her way to the home of a neighbor.

This was something for the law to handle. But (as has been said) the law of Koochiching was in International Falls, a two-day trip away, and the drunken murderer was on the loose, probably armed. In desperation they called the closest lawman they knew of, a deputy sheriff of Itasca County stationed at Bigfork, eleven miles south.

This deputy wasn't much for size, being only about five and a half feet tall. But he was an ex-river-driver, Fred Peloquin, so he didn't scare easily. He got his revolver and came right up.

There wasn't much the callers could tell him. They knew only that the maddened man was somewhere in the forest. Fred went in after him. The deputy found the man, too, but didn't arrest him. The man had killed himself.

Events of this nature aroused a feeling of desperation in the hearts of the sober, sensible people. One of them took time to write this appeal, which was published in the newspapers of the time:

"For God's sake, help us clear Koochiching county of its hundreds of bootlegger joints and stills.

"For God's sake, help us clean up the dives in Craig, Gemmell, Big Falls, and International Falls.

"For God's sake, help us protect law-abiding citizens who are at the mercy of the booze elements which are setting up a kingdom second to Chicago and Herrin.

"For God's sake, help us clean up the hell-hole of Craig, where they knock 'em cold with blunt instruments and tuck the lifeless bodies beneath the ice of the Big Fork River to be washed down with the spring thaws.

"For God's sake, help us in a county where women are beaten to death and the culprits are seldom prosecuted.

"For God's sake, help us protect the innocent and prosecute the crooks, gamblers, resort proprietors, rum runners, intoxicated auto drivers, and wild women.

"For God's sake, help us uphold the spirit of the town marshal at Big Falls, shot down in bold murder at the hands of the element that is endeavoring to do away with Federal patrol of highways in Koochiching.

"For God's sake, help us in our fight to restore law and order in a county which is overrun with illicit booze traffic, where graft and corruption flourish, where the Constitution of the United States is treated as a scrap of paper and the law of the state of Minnesota is taunted." (*Duluth Herald*)

After the repeal of Prohibition, Craig was never as bad as it had been when whiskey could only be obtained from men who were outside the law. But it still was the lumberjack's favorite hangout, and as such was a sort of informal employment agency. Along with International Falls, Bemidji, Virginia, Superior and Duluth, it was a place where men "went down" for their "vacations," and were to be found when they woke up from their bout with drunkenness, broke and hungry. Usually they were happy to be given a ride back to camp, half-sick and sorry, where they would get into shape with a few good hot meals and start accumulating a stake for their next drunk. The barkeepers had no patience with the men when they had spent all their money, and would often phone for someone to come and get them out of their way. Knowing that the old fellows frequently didn't have a friend who would give them that help, the loggers usually obliged.

There were some occupational hazards, though. Frequently the men coming back from their sprees were hung over, and sick, and smelly, and not sober enough to be responsible for their behavior. They meant no harm, but the juice of their Copenhagen when they'd spit out the window stripped the paint off the side of many a boss' car.

During the war, there was a logging camp on each side of Craig, about a mile from the town's lively bars. One logger hired a team of cooks that were soon famous as world-beaters. In order to keep his crew from deserting to the other camp, his competitor was forced to find an equally competent grubslinger. That raised a fresh problem. The men kept walking back and forth from one camp to the other, trying to determine where they would get the best meal; but somehow they never made it all the way. With a riproaring tavern halfway between, offering all kinds of exciting inducements as well as room service, a good share of the crew from both camps got hung up between. Both loggers said it was the most changeable crew they'd ever had.

PICAROON

The most monumental battle I ever witnessed occurred between two partner-brothers who went on a spree together. Whatever started the fracas I don't recall, but it wasn't long before they were swinging at each other. They were both big, tough bruisers, and a haymaker from either one would knock the other back some ten feet, where he'd fetch up against the wall or furniture, and come back swinging. They slugged each other back and forth for some time, and the damage was of epic proportions. Their shirts were torn, their faces banged up, and the furnishings of the tavern were broken and upset. The tavern keeper was dancing about begging them to desist, to have pity on his place, grabbing futilely at their arms. It only made them madder. All their attention was concentrated on their private war, and if the bartender got in their way he was swept aside like an irritating twig in the woods. Their breaths came in great heaving gusts. Presently they began to lay hands on the chairs, tearing them apart and using them as weapons. They broke up the chairs, the tables, the bottles and glasses and whatever else they could seize. The mirror was shattered, the place a shambles, but they kept pounding each other until both were exhausted and one had a broken arm and the other a goose egg on his head as big as a fist. They were practically unconscious when I hauled them back to camp, broke and sick besides.

The ironic sequel was that, since they were cutting partners, the one who had broken his brother's arm now had to work twice as hard, sawing, while the cripped brother used his left arm; and all over something so insignificant it wasn't worth being mad about the next day.

But all that wild life is gone. Craig is a ghost town now. The dilapidated remains of a few tar-papered saloons lurch toward the river, overshadowed by the young growth of brush and trees. The river slips tranquilly on its meandering way, looking innocent, with no hint of its turbulent history.

Eventually all the "ladies" went, and the taverns folded, as the lifestyle in the woods changed. The last leaf on the tree was a lady who drove a Cadillac, and so bedazzled a Minneapolis newspaper writer that he fatuously described her as something of a den mother to the teenagers of the area, who buzzed up to her establishment in search of someplace that didn't mind ignoring a little thing like their being underage.

A curious traveler viewing Craig now sees an eerie row of deserted leaning buildings that slope toward the bridge. Weeds choke the doorways and hide the blank and broken windows. There is no sign of the lusty, brawling spirit that whooped it up in the dingy bars and back rooms. The people who made it that way—the jacks and saloon keepers and women—are long gone, and mostly forgotten.

But in its day, Craig was famous, as far away as Arizona. A traveler from there told me of seeing a Great Northern box car, bearing on its side the familiar mountain goat and the slogan, "See America first." Under it, some unknown lonesome lumberjack had scrawled, "P.S.— *Don't* miss Craigville."